TRULY UNFAMOUS

TALES FROM THE GLORY DAYS OF CANADIAN ROCK MUSIC

KEITH R BROWN

 FriesenPress

Suite 300 - 990 Fort St
Victoria, BC, V8V 3K2
Canada

www.friesenpress.com

ISBN
978-1-5255-7119-0 (Hardcover)
978-1-5255-7120-6 (Paperback)
978-1-5255-7121-3 (eBook)

1. MUSIC, BUSINESS ASPECTS

Distributed to the trade by The Ingram Book Company

CONTENTS

This book is dedicated to
Donald and Terry

FOREWARD

I DON'T THINK I NEEDED a personal influence to develop a love for music. But I had one. Her maiden name was Margaret Rose Armstrong and the earliest memory I have of my mother was when she brought home a yellow Westinghouse radio from Robinson's department store. Mom kept moving the toaster-sized bakelite radio around our basement apartment looking for the best reception. When she set it on the window sill in the kitchen, CHML came in clear as a bell. I remember how happy she was to have music in the house.

There were other childhood memories linking my mother and music. By the age of four I was going to the movies with Mom to see musicals. Her favourite was "Singing in the Rain." A few years later we watched this guy called Elvis doing this new thing called rock 'n roll on the Dorsey Brothers television show. I'm sure Mom would have loved the Beatles. And despite her obsession with trying to keep me out of harm's way, I'd like to think she would have made an exception when I decided I wanted to work in the music business.

Obviously music was at the heart of my career choice. But I had another motivation. From the age of twelve, I always had a year-round part-time job, usually at supermarket or a restaurant. Early on, I knew how it felt to look at the clock and silently groan, wondering if this shift was ever going to end. However, one evening in 1965, the high school had a career night and one of the guest speakers fired my imagination. He was a copywriter at a radio station. He described how sometimes when we was doing his job, he would look at the clock and wonder how the time had passed so *quickly*.

How can I get a job like that? It's said that if you find the right line of work, you may never work day in your life.

I had no plan for attaining this dream career until a guidance councillor told me about a school in Montreal called Loyola College. It offered a Bachelor's Degree in Communication Arts. If I had something like that in my resume, who knows what kind of work I might find? This is what drew me to the gloriously playground which was Montreal in the late sixties.

While I was study filmmaking, several specific things happened which caused me to drift into the music business. But an important underlying factor was something I didn't notice at the time. During my final semester, the government passed broadcast regulations forcing radio stations start playing more Canadian music. These new rules spurred investments in artists, labels, recordings, and studios. Along with the wave of new of artists, there would be a much larger wave of people working behind the scenes. I would become one them.

Initially (that is, for the next ten years), I worked as a concert promoter. Eventually I would help create Canada's first national tour circuit for rock bands during the emergence of "arena rock." I toured the groups from St. John's, Newfoundland, to Prince Rupert, British Columbia, 4700 miles away. Some years I would crisscross the country numerous times. The longest continuous tour I put together stopped in over eighty different markets. April Wine, The Stampeders, B.T.O, Triumph and Rush are just some of the more recognizable Canadian names I presented in Canadian hockey rinks. But I also had notable encounters with the Bee Gees, the Rolling Stones, Brian Wilson and many more. This book is about some of my experiences.

Because I was truly "un-famous" in a business where fame is the name of the game, I never thought I would ever write a book about my career. However, the as I read the many rock 'n roll memoirs which have been published lately, I began to draw a different take. Maybe being "truly unfamous" has the advantage of having no image to maintain and what Bob Dylan described as "…no secrets to conceal."

So here's the story of the first of the first decade in the Canadian music business. Like the routing of some of my concert tours, "Truly Unfamous" is a journey with its share of side-tracking, back-tracking and the occasional walk in the woods. But the one constant is the music. A great many people I met along the way are no longer with us. More than anything else, it's for them that I wrote this book.

CHAPTER ONE

LAUGH-IN

IN THE SUMMER OF 1969, I was entering my second year at college in Montreal. I lived on my own. Government loans and bursaries more than covered school costs, but I needed extra income for food and bad habits.

I was the bassist in a band called The Floyd Jones Group. We might earn a hundred bucks a gig, two or three times a month and though this helped to make ends meet, I didn't think we were destined for greatness. My hope was the band might open doors and in a way I couldn't have imagined, that's exactly what happened.

I spent the best part of a year on a winding path which would eventually lead me to a bar called Laugh-In.

When The Floyd Jones Group entered *The 1968 C-FOX-Donald K Donald Battle of the Bands,* we were on the very bottom rung of Donald K Donald Agency's talent roster. Donald sold these "battles", complete with radio promotion on C-FOX AM radio, for a few hundred dollars to local pro-moters. The bands were paid with "exposure" so Donald didn't have to pay them with cash. It's no wonder he kept adding additional rounds. Floyd Jones was in so many "battles", we were eventually able to negotiate a twenty-dollar-per-show travel allowance.

As the contest kept getting extended, we developed a competitive advantage; better bands joined the musicians' union and had to drop out. Since Donald's contest didn't pay, the union wouldn't let their members participate. By the time we finally made it to the finals, there was only one other group from the first round; Red Power. They were four Mohawks from the Kahnawake Reserve, just south of Montreal. In terms of skill, we were comparable. But because we played a lot of original material, we won.

We were awarded three prizes. One was a package of Shure products, so we got some nice new microphones. The second was a recording session at the new RCA Studios although when we showed up, there was no engineer. By the time one was found, there was only time to cut two demos. The final prize, the one which really would have made a difference, was $5,000 in bookings from Donald K Donald. But when I went to the agency to ask about it, they told me steady bookings would only start to materialize in the fall. However, if I wanted, there was a position open for janitor and dishwasher at Donald's bar, Laugh-In.

It turns out that a thirty-dollar-a-week job mopping floors, cleaning washrooms, and washing beer glasses was a door to the music business which Floyd Jones opened.

JIM-CARRIERS

The first show I worked at The Montreal Forum was a Doors concert. It was 1969 and the stagehands' union had yet to make it into the building. As the promoter of the show, Donald K Donald, had to recruit the stagehands. I was given the day off from my job at Laugh-In, and Donald would even paying me ten bucks. I would have done it for free.

It took us three to four hours to load-in and set-up all the gear. When we were done, The Doors' stage manager pulled me aside and asked if I wanted to be a "Jim-Carrier." I had no idea what that meant, but I was game. I was told I'd need an assistant and we would be getting all-access crew passes which included free refreshments.

I recruited my friend Oleh and we were soon introduced to The Doors' crew. They asked us to take part in a pool they had going. Five bucks would buy a number between one and twelve which represented the numbers on the face of a clock. At the end of the show, Jim Morrison would attempt a headstand in the middle of the stage. We were betting on the direction he'd fall; twelve o'clock was towards the audience. Five dollars was half our day's wage, but we weren't going to pass this up.

After the second opening act was done, we were to report to the monitor mixing board next to the stage. There we would learn what it meant to be a "Jim-Carrier." Turns out it was pretty obvious; our job was to *carry Jim Morrison* from the dressing room to the stage and back after the show.

They brought us to the Doors' dressing room and showed us how to link our hands to make a throne for the Lizard King. Soon, we heard the crowd roar which meant they must have dimmed the house lights. And just like that, Jim Morrison climbed onto our interlocked arms and we headed towards the stage. He was much lighter than I expected.

The sounds of the crowd kept getting louder as we walked down the corridor and when we turned out towards the rink, the crowd erupted. I could feel the audience in my lungs. We got to the stage and lift up Jim Morrison handing him off to the crew onstage. Our job done, we turned to leave and watch the show. But the monitor guy told us Jim-Carriers had to stay right next to him, just off stage. We soon learned why.

About five songs into the set, Jim let out a signature scream and tossed his head back so forcefully he fell and struck the back of his skull on a tuning key someone had left in the bass drum. He looked stunned. The stage techs ran onstage, picked him up and called us into action, "Jim-Carriers, Jim-Carriers!" like this was something that happen all the time.

We shuttled him back to the dressing room. The tour manager parted his hair to sponge off the blood while Jim killed a bottle of Miller High Life. Before we knew it, he was bandaged up, back on our arms, and we were headed to the stage where the three other Doors were playing an extended jam.

The rest of the show went smoothly. And at the end of the encore, Jim Morrison attempted a headstand. He landed at three o'clock.

A BAR CALLED LAUGH-IN

If "Laugh-In" sounds familiar, it's probably because the bar took its name from a famous sketch-comedy TV show. But Laugh-In the bar featured music, not comedy. The walls resembled the back-drops used on the TV show but this was the only connection I could ever make between the two.

The bar itself was small. It had a fire limit of eighty-seven, which was often exceeded, and the stage was just big enough for a ping pong table but too small to actually play a game. It was upstairs from a well-known club called Café Andre.

Café Andre had a weird ambiance. It was a folk music club, but it had linen tablecloths, candles, and tuxedoed waiters. This might have been the way you run a folk club in Paris, but in Montreal it was weird. Performers at Café Andre like

David Wiffen and Dee Higgins, preferred to walk upstairs to hang out at Laugh-In between sets.

There were a lot of things I liked about Laugh-In. I especially liked the manager, Tom Hansen. He had worked in an office for several years, but in his mid-twenties decided to leave the nine-to-five and run away to the circus that was Laugh-In. Between his sense of humour and charm, he easily made friends with all kinds of people. Within a week of me starting, Tom decided I should tend bar so he could spend more time socializing with our patrons.

Laugh-In's three owners were Donald (K Donald) Tarlton, Terry Flood, and Bob Lemm. Terry and Donald would often wear suede jackets and polyester shirts, looking like they had walked straight out of the Rat Pack's closet. Bob Lemm was a bit older and looked like a beatnik, the precursor to hippies (or "heads" as we preferred to be called), and fit in perfectly with most of Laugh-In's young clientele.

I think Bob Lemm liked owning a bar that was funnier than the TV show it was named after. Donald saw Laugh-In as a tool that could help promote his DKD brand. Terry Flood hoped Laugh-In would make money.

Donald implemented several policies that almost guaranteed Terry's plan would fail. The first allowed any musician on the roster of the Donald K Donald Agency to run a tab at Laugh-In and buy drinks at special "musicians' prices." That meant a cold bottle of beer was sold at cost (a quarter) and hard liquor with a mix was forty-five cents. Even in the late sixties, this was a great deal.

To give you an example of how crazy this got, a diminutive drummer named Richard Cezar had the distinction of running the biggest tab at Laugh-In. When the word came down to close Richard's account, it was sitting at $1400 which was roughly 5600 Molson Exports. A couple of months later,

Richard's guitarist, who didn't really drink, somehow had his tab hit the $1200 mark.

On weekends, musicians were usually off performing somewhere which left space for "civilians" to buy drinks at regular price. That helped with our cash-flow. But Sunday through Thursday, the place was filled with off-duty musicians.

The bar was quickly becoming a legion hall for the best players in Montreal's rock community. I got to know many remarkable people I still know today.

Another policy Donald implemented allowed any announcer at a Montreal rock radio station to drink *for free*. Because of this, Donald developed incredible relationships with Montreal's top D.J.s.

I was serving up free drinks to amazing characters, the deejays who played rock music on Montreal radio in 1969 and 1970, most of whom were celebrities in their own right. I even had a chance to befriend some of them and quickly learnt how the radio game was played.

MONTREAL ROCK RADIO IN 1969

Most of the customers at Laugh-In were real people with real jobs in the real world and presumably, they came to Laugh-In because of the bands. We referred to them as "civilians." The second-largest contingent, especially on weeknights, were band members. But the most vocal and memorable customers, the ones who gave Laugh-In that remarkable ambiance, were the radio announcers.

Radio jocks were entertainers. They had large audiences but when the good ones were at work, it was like they were speaking only to you. Each announcer had his own distinctive style, but there were two types of announcers.

An AM radio announcer was a *performer*. AM Top 40 radio had very strict limits on which songs could be played since it promised "All of the Hits; All of the Time." Any spontaneity came because AM jocks wanted everyone to laugh at their jokes and buy into characters, which might be very different from their off-the-mic personalities.

The FM guys were about keeping it real, in the sense they wanted to share their love of music, especially within their own "tribe." Each announcer could express his personal musical taste and many of the albums in the library were green-lighted from start to finish. And they practiced what they preached. For example, CHOM-FM, Montreal's FM rock station, had an unwritten policy that smoking dope was *only* allowed on the third floor.

When the FM guys came into the bar, they were very much like their on-air personalities and could spend hours talking to you about music. By contrast, the real personalities of the AM guys could be uncharacteristic.

One guy who was warm and fuzzy with his listeners was darker and funnier than Lenny Bruce. Another who was Mr. Nice Guy on air might try to slap things out with someone at the bar. These brief flair-ups were the only violence we had at Laugh-In.

Some were *serious* drinkers. One of them always asked me for white rum; not a single or a double, but a bottle of Barcardi Light. He might share it with some girl at the bar, but normally he'd drain the bottle, all on his own.

Getting to know all of these characters certainly enhanced my radio listening experience. I started hearing in-jokes and could appreciate the irony of jocks making fun of their own on-air characters. Radio DJs are a fraternity and although I could never be a member, working at Laugh-In taught me the secret handshake.

ON ANY GIVEN NIGHT

Another policy Donald implemented was that anyone who was performing at the Montreal Forum would have an open bar and open mic at Laugh-In. It didn't take long for us to become the unofficial after-party venue for some of Montreal's top concerts.

Donavan, most of Blood Sweat and Tears, The Doors (less Jim Morrison – who had a headache that night), Jethro Tull, Steppenwolf, and The Guess Who all played free shows at Laugh-In.

Our main entrance was on the second floor and halfway up the stairs was a landing with a small brass plaque that paid tribute to the lead singer of the Guess Who. It had an arrow pointing to the floor with an inscription, "Burton Cummings Barfed Here."

We always kept a bottle of champagne in the fridge for Andy Kim, the man who wrote "Sugar Sugar" for The Archies, not to mention a string of his own international hits. Whenever he was there, he would crack open a bottle and pass it around. But we were a beer crowd.

Some Saturday nights, Jim McKenna, the host of the teen dance program, *Like Young*, would be our guest bartender. He had recruited Tom and I to help out as talent coordinators for his show, and after Saturday evening tapings, Jim would accompany us back to the club. He would then spend hours behind the bar pouring drinks and appealing for tips, which he would always give to me.

One Sunday, Tom Hansen asked if I could go check on a slightly crazy-looking guy sitting by himself. He had nothing but a glass of soda and Tommy wanted to make sure he was OK. It turned out Ted Nugent wasn't OK. The night before, he had disbanded The Amboy Dukes because the drummer had thrown a cymbal into the audience, injuring a girl. The band stood up for the drummer, so he fired them all. That night, nursing a club soda, Ted was wondering if it was worth continuing. Though it was my day off, I settled into my role as barman/consoler and asked him what he could see himself doing if he wasn't a rock guitarist. Ted thought about it long and hard, but didn't have an answer.

Some big names played Laugh-In. But, week in and week out, it was the Canadian acts that packed the place. The Modern Rock Quartet (M.R.Q.) from Ottawa, SOMA from Halifax, Chilliwack from Vancouver, Energy from Montreal (featuring a drummer named Corky Laing, who would soon join a new group called Mountain), Crowbar from Hamilton, and Steel River from Toronto were just a few of the bands that commanded our little stage.

One of the most popular attractions was George Oliver and Natural Gas. I first saw George in the Rogues when I was living in Burlington, Ontario, and saw him again with The Mandala when I was living in Ottawa. I was already a fan when he rolled into Laugh-In with his new band, Natural Gas.

Laugh-In, with its $500/week cap for band fees, wasn't George's idea of a great gig. But like most musicians, the guys in Natural Gas loved playing the club. The band had a very likeable road manager named Robbie who negotiated a compromise. When the band came to Montreal, they would alternate between Laugh-In and Le Boulevard de Paris (which would pay George three or four times our fee.) One time, when Natural Gas played Le Boulevard, we closed early so our staff and customers could walk over to St-Catherine Street to catch George's last set.

The staff, musicians, and regulars all became quite close. When the weather was nice, we might go up on the roof to smoke joints and watch the glimmering lights of downtown

Montreal. For a while Tom kept a chicken on the roof, mostly so he could ask female customers, "Do you want to see my pet chicken?"

One of my favourite moments at Laugh-in involved one of our waiters named Paul. Paul was probably the only person at Laugh-In who didn't seem to care much about music. He was there for two things: weekend tips and women. He would often boast that he could go home with any available woman. The other waiters would often make bets with him on whether he would succeed.

This one week, the celebrated blues guitarist Johnny Winter was there with The Johnny Winter And... band, rehearsing for their official debut on a bill which featured Van Morrison, Jethro Tull, and Jefferson Airplane. This was the band that recorded Johnny's biggest radio hit, "Rock and Roll Hoochie Koo".

Johnny was an albino. He wasn't very tall and had a slight build. He also had long platinum blonde hair that framed slightly crossed eyes and a prominent nose.

That night, Paul was his usual self, surveying the room for prospects. His eyes landed on a slender figure with long blonde hair seated, facing away from us, at the end of the room.

"Check out that blonde," Paul said.

We all smiled. One of the other waiters said, "If you like that, wait till you see the face."

"Who wants to bet I can get her number?"

There was no way, we assured him. He was out of his league. Biting our tongues, we gladly took the bet.

Paul began clearing empties from tables as he made his way to the end of the room where he placed his hand on the shoulder of Johnny's green velvet jacket and asked, "Hey Gorgeous, what can I get for you?"

The blonde turned and Paul was now face-to-face with the slightly cross-eyed prominent-nosed Johnny Winter. Shocked, Paul staggered backwards and dropped his tray of empties. Everyone in the bar turned to look and started applauding. Even Johnny, who wasn't in on the joke, laughed.

One night, a months or so later, the staff went The Hawaiian Lounge to check out the last set by David Foster's band Night Train. Paul spent all his time dancing with a man who looked like Cher. By last call, Laugh-In's lady-killer decided he was turning over a new leaf.

THE TRIANGLE TO MASHMAKHAN

There were two Canadian bands that would have people lining up on the stairs, outside the door, and down the street. One was George and Natural Gas, and the other was The Triangle.

Originally called Trevor Payne and the Triangle, the band felt they could do without the huge personality of their frontman Trevor Payne. They had learned how to entertain a crowd and had a strong set of original songs written by the organist, Pierre Senecal. They were ready to go out on their own.

The Triangle quickly became the most popular English band in Montreal. Pierre, did most of the lead vocals and played the Hammond B-3 using foot pedals for the band's bass parts. He was supported by Rayburn Blake on guitar and Jerry Mercer on drums, who fell into Trevor's role as the band's showman.

The highlight of Jerry's performances was always the drum solo. At its climax, the stage lights blacked-out as a strobe light started flashing above his shaved head. It would look like streams of intense light were radiating from his sweat-glistened scalp. For the next twenty years, including when he played with April Wine, Jerry's nickname was "Beamer."

Late one afternoon during my first week at Laugh-In, Jerry was practicing on stage while I was mopping the floors. He had something he wanted to get off his chest. At the time, he had a great day-job at IBM. The money was good, there was insurance, a retirement plan, and tons of room for advancement. But the band was taking up a lot of his time. The Triangle was popular but only in Montreal. He needed to make a choice.

His girlfriend Linda was pushing for the IBM option and it made sense. He was good at the job and his head was into it. But his heart was with the band. I didn't quite know what to say but I suggested if I had even the smallest fraction of his talent, I would want to find out where this music thing might lead. This may have been exactly what he wanted to hear. I think he just needed a little moral support and, being Jerry, it didn't matter if it was coming from a guy who was washing floors.

It was while they were still playing regularly at Laugh-In that The Triangle signed a recording contract with Columbia Records in Toronto.

The label saw the band as a work in progress and insisted they needed an additional singer; one who had no trace of a French accent and could play bass. The band chose Brian Edwards, whose older brother, Cliff Edwards, was one of two lead singers in a pop group called The Bells.

Also, The Triangle needed a new name. They were no longer a trio and there already was a recording act called The Triangle. The band came up with "Mashmakhan", which was a kind of Jamaican pot.

They recorded their debut album in New York where at one point, the label brought in Bernard Purdy to drum on some tracks. And after all of that, Columbia decided there was no single on the album. But in a suite they recorded called "Shades of Loneliness", there was an upbeat section of the nine-minute piece that was edited to be used as a B-side. It was entitled "As the Years Go By."

This little-B-side-that-could almost cracked the American Top 30 and sold half a million copies stateside. It was even more surprising when the track went on to become the second biggest foreign single in Japan that year, narrowly edged out by "Bridge Over Troubled Water". It sold over a million copies and was a #1 hit in both Canada and Japan.

Mashmakhan was invited to join the Festival Express, a movable musical feast starring the Grateful Dead, Janis Joplin and The Band which crossed the country in a chartered fourteen-car CN train. Some of their most memorable performances were during this tour as can be seen in the 2003 documentary *Festival Express*.

For their second album, the band retreated to Jamaica to record. There, they enjoyed the local strain of their namesake and had the idea of democratizing the songwriting process. Pierre was no longer in charge of writing all the songs; everyone would get a shot.

The album that resulted, *The Family*, was a complete failure. The original group disbanded soon afterward.

EARLY VINTAGE APRIL WINE

I've heard various stories about how April Wine wound up in Montreal. One involves a singer and employee in the D.K.D. office named Harrison Tabb who responded to a demo. Another version involves Halifax entrepreneur Peter Christakos introducing Donald and Terry to the band. There was even a story the band used to tell in interviews about heading for the "promised land" of Toronto from Halifax, but running out of money by the time they got to Montreal.

One thing is certain. April Wine, before they recorded *April Wine*, turned up at Laugh-In looking for work.

The club was usually booked at least a month in advance so while they waited their turn, the DKD office directed them to a rooming house at the foot of Crescent Street called The Inn. Shortly afterwards, they were fixed up with a cottage near St-Sauveur, an hour north of the city.

When April Wine finally got their booking, I remember thinking they were okay. Compared to many of the other bands that played Laugh-In, they weren't great musicians, but they had interesting original material.

Three of the four guys in the band had the last name "Henman." Drummer Ritchie and guitarist David were brothers, while the bass player, Jimmy, was their cousin. The non-Henman was the other guitarist, Miles Goodwin. (This isn't a typo, he would later change the "I's" to "Y's.")

Unlike the Henmans, Myles wasn't so outgoing. He usually wore a black leather jacket and seemed to prefer sitting at any spot at the bar with an empty stool on either side. The Henmans were always approachable. Myles, not so much.

Everyone in the band was a songwriter and all did some singing, but the lead vocalists were David and Jimmy Henman. Myles, the voice that would eventually lead the band to stardom, wanted to concentrate on guitar and tended to be a bit of a "shoe-gazer" on-stage. This would soon change, and it happened because of Laugh-In.

Donald, Terry, and Bob had started a label called Aquarius Records which would later sign April Wine. But the first album they released was by a band called Freedom North which often played the club. The first single from Aquarius to ever play on the radio was Freedom North's, "Doctor Tom" which was a tribute to Tom Hansen and the way he could "make things good tonight." The leader of the band was a guitarist named Bill Hill who also owned an eight-track studio called Montreal Sound. Billy was hired to produce April Wine's debut album.

In the studio, it became apparent to Billy that Jimmy Henman, one of April Wine's lead vocalists, tended to sing slightly flat a bit too often. This wasn't so obvious live, but it very noticeable in the studio. Billy asked Myles to try singing lead vocals. Myles' voice had a unique vibrato and sweet tonality. Plus, his pitch was fine. As a result, April Wine's first single, "Fast Train", was sung by Myles Goodwyn (now spelled with "Ys") and not their frontman to date, Jimmy.

After April Wine made its debut album, Jimmy Henman didn't seem the same. He was like someone whose dog had run away. It's easy to suppose his relegation to back-up vocals was his reason for leaving the band and returning to Halifax. But I also heard Jimmy felt the lifestyle of a rock musician conflicted with his Christian values. In any case, Jimmy Henman went to college and became a teacher.

When April Wine came to Laugh-In, they were four guys from Nova Scotia looking for a recording deal. By the end of Laugh-In, they were on their way to becoming one of Canada's most memorable homegrown bands. But we'll get to that later.

THE PARK AVENUE PANSIES

One night my girlfriend, Brenda, introduced me to some gentlemen who showed up at the bar. They didn't look anything like our hippie patrons. These guys looked like Sinatra fans from New Jersey. Brenda suggested they might be useful to have around. But when I asked what they did for a living, she told me I probably didn't want to know. We came to know them as the Park Avenue Pansies.

In one of my first encounters with them, Norm, their leader, motioned me over and said he didn't appreciate Terry staring at him. Norm, Roy the Ostrich and Big Abby were sitting at the bar. Terry, who was across the room, kept looking at them. Norm told me he could get Terry and Donald to leave and asked if I wanted to play along. I had no reason for wanting Terry or Donald to leave, but I thought if there was any bad blood with The Pansies, things might not end well. I was also curious about what he had in mind.

All I had to do was not turn on the taped music when the band finished their set. And so when the band wrapped up, I stayed behind the bar. That's when Norm and Roy started an oddly conspicuous conversation.

"This place would be really easy to knock over," said Norm. Roy agreed.

Big Abby asked, "How much money do you think is in the cash?"

"Probably not so much," said Norm, "but nobody here is using credit cards. There must be a few hundred."

There were speaking loud enough to ensure Terry would hear. And sure enough, he immediately summoned Tom Hansen to a meeting over by the washrooms. Tom told me to empty the cash from the till into a paper bag and bring it to the back-door downstairs.

Just as Norm had planned, Donald, Terry, and Tom quickly left the club. When I got back to the bar, Norm gave me a nod.

As time went by, The Pansies helped us out when less-friendly types showed up offering protection (and a new cigarette machine). During football season, the staff even played touch football against The Pansies Sunday mornings on Fletcher's Field. That's how we found out why Roy was called "The Ostrich." He was so fast and elusive he could score at will. The Pansies were an incongruous, but welcome, part of the club's atmosphere. However, one night, things got weird.

Big Abby was the obvious muscle of the Pansies. He looked a little like Sam Huff, the all-star middle linebacker for the New York Giants, except Abby might have been bigger. He did various jobs, but it seemed his bread and butter was collecting money for loan sharks.

One night, Abby entered Laugh-In on crutches with his leg in a cast and bruises on his face. He hobbled over to the bar, ordered a Molson Ex, then another and another. By about eleven o'clock Abby was swaying and ready to move on. But as he rose from his stool, he stumbled and fell. I hurried around the bar to help him up.

"I don't need your fuckin' help, smart guy," he blurted. I went back behind the bar but Abby was still glaring at me. He motioned me over.

"Get me my overcoat," he growled.

It was the middle of summer and must have been about 80 degrees that night. I asked Abby if he was sure he had an overcoat. Bad idea.

He reached into his sports jacket, pulled a revolver out of his shoulder holster and stuck it in my face. In a matter of seconds, everyone at the bar was somewhere else.

Abby slowly repeated, "Get me my overcoat."

I didn't really think my old pal Abby was about to shoot me in the face. But then again, I *was* staring down the barrel of a gun.

"OK Abby, I'm just going to look in the kitchen where the coat rack is."

He nodded and I went back to the kitchen to figure out what I would do next. I figured he'd just get more upset if I ignored him, so my lame solution was to go back out there and suggest that somebody must have taken his overcoat by accident. I told him I would ask the waiters if they saw anybody leave with it.

"It's bound to show up", I assured him.

Abby put his gun away and said, "I'll be back tomorrow to get my coat, understand?"

He turned around and in a slow lumbering manner, hobbled out of the club.

I thought that would be the end of it. But at the beginning of the following evening there was Abby's large frame filling the club's entrance. He took a seat at his favourite stool. I explained I still needed a little more time to find his coat.

He waved me off, "Forget about that."

Reaching into his pocket he pulled out a set of car keys and placed them on the bar. "This is for you."

"What's this?" I asked.

"I dunno, a Buick or an Oldsmobile or something like that. It's in the back alley."

"But Abby, I don't even drive", I lied.

"Then give it to a friend, but I want you to forget about last night."

Taking the keys I said, "Abby, I don't even know what you're talking about."

"Damn right," he said.

I offered him a beer but he said he had to be going. I went down to the alley and sure enough, there was a late-model Buick. If I thought for one moment it wasn't stolen, I would have at least taken it for a spin. Instead, I put the keys in the ignition and went back upstairs to call the police about a parked car which was blocking the alley.

THE END OF LAUGH-IN

Laugh-In never actually had its own liquor license. As far as the Regie d'Alcools de Quebec (the liquor licensing board for Quebec) was concerned, we were the upstairs room of Café Andre.

We bought all of our liquor and beer through an arrangement with Café Andre's very dignified manager, Doris. I expect the Café's owner, Monsieur Racicot, didn't like all the commotion we caused. Though I'm sure he appreciated the impressive volume discounts we were generating from the beer suppliers.

However, it wasn't our liquor arrangement that did us in. The beginning of the end for Laugh-In was the one and only time we were raided by cops.

The authorities were targeting underage customers and there were few nights we didn't have at least a couple of patrons carrying fake IDs. Though the Quebec drinking age had dropped from nineteen to eighteen, we knew some of our customers were even younger.

Even so, I don't recall a single drunk teenager at the club, ever. The kids were alright. They knew they were being allowed into a special place and behaved better than the famous musicians and radio DJs, some of whom were old enough to be their parents.

But they were still illegal and the night the police arrived, I think three or four of them got nabbed. This represented thousands of dollars in fines for the club but a potentially more serious incident involved a waiter, Little Bill, who had about half an ounce of hash. When the police showed up, he panicked and pulled the stash from his pocket and tossed it. Unfortunately, it hit a cop in the leg. Little Bill spent the night at Station 10. But since his dad was a Westmount city councillor, the charges were dropped.

After the raid, the owners decided to close the club for renovations. For the next couple of weeks Bob Lemm, the waiters, and even several of our customers showed up every day to steam off the old wallpaper and install a new stainless-steel dance floor. Bob Lemm's new design looked clean and modern and when we re-opened, Laugh-In was cooler than ever and still packed with the same happy crowd. Vibe-wise, nothing had really changed, except it was now called Tommy's.

As 1970 drew to an end, we learned M. Racicot was selling the building to some people who wanted to open a Greek restaurant. The glorious experiment that was Laugh-in/Tommy's was over. We might have had a lease, but without a liquor license, the jig was up. After the raid, there was no chance of getting our own liquor permit.

Anyone who ever went to Laugh-In (or Tommy's) was lucky. It was one of those places which only could have existed at that time and place.

The most significant event for Donald must have been meeting the woman who would become his wife and partner for life, Ann Warnock.

For Terry, Laugh-In was where a decades-long association with Myles Goodwyn began.

Tom Hansen would have many reasons to think it never got better than Laugh-In, but I'm sure the most significant occurrence for him was meeting the love of his life; Blanche. Tommy and Blanche would marry, raise two children and play a crucial role in my own story.

For me, Laugh-In was just as life-changing. Aside from being my second home for well over a year, I learned a lot about radio, about musicians, and about problem-solving. Far more than getting a Bachelor's degree in film-making, working at Laugh-In established my career path.

CHAPTER TWO

THE ACID DAYS

IT ALWAYS SEEMED ODD TO me that Bryan Adams wrote "The Summer of '69." After all, in the summer of 1969 Bryan was only nine years old. I had just turned twenty and will always remember it for some of the best days of my life. Shakespeare coined the phrase *salad days* in reference to a time of youthful enthusiasm and indiscretion. The Bard could have been talking about my summer of 1969, although a truer description might be "Acid Days."

MAGIC DUROCHER GARDENS

Though I was spending sixty hours a week at Laugh-In, there were plenty of other things happening in my life. For one thing, there was Loyola. Loyola College was an English Jesuit college which eventually merged with Sir George Williams University to form Concordia University.

At the time, my tuition was about $600 and between used textbooks, eating, and paying rent, I was spending more than the $1200 I got each year from the federal government. The rest I covered by playing in The Floyd Jones Group and working at Laugh-In.

Half of what the Canadian government gave me came in the form of a loan, and the other half as a bursary, meaning so long as I graduated, I wouldn't have to pay it back. That wasn't the only reason I finished my studies. I genuinely enjoyed learning. Studying theology, French philosophers (in French), and Greek drama probably wasn't very useful. Majoring in filmmaking could have just been an excuse to get stoned and watch lots of movies. But the Jesuit heritage of Loyola instilled a way of thinking that challenges every new idea and changed the way I looked at life.

I lived in a place known as the "Magic Durocher Gardens" in what's called the McGill Ghetto. "The Ghetto" was where many McGill University students from all across Canada and from around the world found cheap residences. There was also a large contingency of Americans who were trying to avoid dying in Vietnam. On any given day, you would see hippies walking past draft dodgers on their way to a biker bar to buy drugs. Today, the people have changed and so have rental prices, but the hilly streets, leafy sidewalks, and old stone buildings still make it an incredible place to live.

I first discovered "The Ghetto" on a warm summer evening while trying to escape the madness of downtown Montreal. My friend Robert and I had drifted into this beautifully serene, comforting, neighbourhood. The Ghetto welcomed us with a warm embrace like we were its prodigal children returning to the shire. Sure, we were also tripping on acid; but that doesn't mean the feeling wasn't real, man.

A week later, I rented a spacious three-room unit on the third floor of the Durocher Apartments.

The floors were warped, and the walls were paper-thin. The bathroom door banged into the toilet when opening it, and the closet-sized kitchen was home to a large family of cockroaches. But it had a living room, a good-sized bedroom, three big windows that opened onto the tall leafy trees outside. Another attraction was the rent was fifteen dollars a week.

The great location and low rent didn't just attract college kids. The "Magic Durocher Gardens" was home to a whole community of fantastic characters. Next door lived a middle-aged gay couple who enjoyed drinking, yelling in French, and sometimes threatening each other with knives. Down the hall lived some exotic dancers and downstairs there was a music critic with the Montreal Star who lived next door to a geriatric couple. One summer, teenagers from the affluent suburb of Town of Mount Royal took the apartment below mine so they could spend their summer vacation shooting crystal meth. Seeing their endless summer of physical degeneration was a bit off-putting but still, I loved the place.

Having moved into my new apartment in a new part of the city, I felt things were falling into place. I had a job I loved, was doing well in school, and though I didn't have a TV, I had a half-decent stereo to play all my music. I figured the next right-of-passage would be to get a phone.

A phone line cost $8.90 a month, which basically increased the price of me staying there by 15%. And though I knew this wasn't cheap, I didn't expect to be the only tenant in the entire building to have a telephone.

Soon, people would come over just to use it. There was a girl from down the hall who had to call her mom because she was pregnant and wanted to come home. When she admitted she wasn't sure who the father was, her mom told her she was on her own. There was a "head" from the second floor who needed the phone so he could obsessively, and unsuccessfully, try to convince his "old lady" (what we call girlfriends back then), to please come back. One time an actual old lady from downstairs knocked on my door to ask if she could call the police because her husband had died.

There was a group of drug dealers who lived in the basement. They were friendly enough so long as they didn't dislike you and I actually became good friends with the smallest and youngest member of that group, a self-professed Casanova named Ducky. Ducky lost a hand as a kid in Halifax when he fell under a streetcar. But if he ever felt sorry for himself, I never saw it. He'd spend a lot of his time up in my apartment talking to his legion of lady-friends on my phone. However, we'd also smoke some of his stash while listening to records on my stereo.

The nicest apartment in the building belonged to Bob and his old lady Caroline. They were always burning incense and an hour never passed without somebody rolling a spliff. Their apartment was decked out exactly how you'd picture a hippie den in 1969; coloured light-bulbs, beaded curtains, black-light posters, and a large hookah on a low table covered with a madras-patterned cloth. People constantly stopped by to pick up some hash, drink some tea, and discuss real spiritual topics, ranging from Madame Blavatsky to Samsara to Jimi Hendrix.

There was a young aspiring musician who would hang out at the apartment and play Bob's Gibson SG for hours on end. Bob had been in a band called The Beat Boys and was somewhat of a role model for this young man. Also, the Gibson was probably the best guitar this kid could get is hands on at the time. His name was Frank Marino.

If you've never heard of Frank Marino, he is one of Canada's most talented rock guitarists and had a band called Mahogany Rush. To give you an idea of how good he was, there is a popular myth that during an acid trip, he was visited by the spirit of Jimi Hendrix. And when he came down,

Frank was able to play like him. In reality, Frank practiced the guitar every day from the age of twelve. The Frank I remember, who must have been fourteen at the time, would spend hours trying to nail a clean A-major chord, using just his middle finger; he was a stickler for that high open-E. Frank was trying to perfect something at the age of fourteen that many professional guitarists don't do their entire careers.

A few months into my stay at Durocher, my band-leader, Stanley Frank, suggested he should move in with me and pay half the rent. He was also a fellow Loyola student and was always strapped for cash. If we split the rent, it would be one dollar a day for each of us, which seemed like a great idea. I had also hoped that we could maybe work on some of The Floyd Jones Group's songs together, but unfortunately not. Stan worked alone. Even at a dollar a day, Stan had trouble paying his half of the rent. However, he was very good at pointing out when I was full of shit – an insight which, at that stage in my life, had value.

The Magic Durocher Gardens had a profound impact on my life. Laugh-In taught me about the music business, Loyola taught me how to question everything, and The Gardens taught me how to get along with just about anyone. During my time there, I did a lot of acid, ate a lot of boiled eggs (they were the only thing cockroaches couldn't get into), met my fellow Jim-Carrier and closest friend to this day, Oleh, and lived the real life of a "head."

WOODSTOCK: THREE DAYS OF PEACE AND MUSIC

I only took a vacation once while staying at The Gardens. Besides never having more than just enough money to get by, there wasn't any place I wanted to go. However, in the summer of '69, handbills for something called the "Woodstock Music and Art Fair" began appearing around the McGill Student Ghetto. "Three Days of Peace and Music" promised to be my kind of weekend.

Tommy agreed to give me some time off so I packed a sleeping bag, took a city bus to the Verdun on-ramp near the Champlain Bridge, and hitchhiked south to Woodstock. It took a couple of rides to make it to the border. My last lift in Canada left me just short so I had to walk the final mile or so. When I arrived at U.S. Customs and Immigration in Champlain, New York, on foot, I was told hitchhikers weren't allowed to enter the United States unless they already had a ride. There would be hundreds of cars crossing that morning headed to Woodstock so I asked if it would be okay if someone agreed to take me.

The Customs officer pointed to an area where cars were being pulled over and the passengers interviewed. I could try my luck there and if I could find someone to take me within an hour, I'd be on my way south. The border was different back then.

Quite a few carloads of hippies headed to Woodstock were pulled over. I offered them all same advice: if they had any "smoking dope", the customs guys would find it. No matter where they tried to hide it, the border guards would find it.

Before I knew it, I was holding weed for two different parties being interrogated in the nearby office. While I was waiting for them to return, three other "heads" returning to their car came up to me and said I should go with them.

"But I have to return a bunch of pot," I explained.

"No, we heard them talking about you," they said nodding to the customs office. "They were getting ready to send you back so we said we'd take you."

Ten minutes later we were cruising down I-87 rolling joints with weed I'd scored for free at a U.S. government facility mere yards inside the border.

A few weeks earlier, the town of Woodstock had cancelled the festival but the organizers managed to move the venue to Yasgur's farm near the town of Bethel. We were a few miles out, near White Lake, when we were stopped by state troopers. The town of Bethel itself was overwhelmed and the troopers were stopping all traffic from getting any closer. I thanked my new buddies for the lift, hopped out of the car and continued on foot. It was Friday evening.

By the time I reached Bethel, it started drizzling and the sky was getting dark. I walked past a small tent village near town and met three students from the University of Pittsburgh looking to score some weed. I said that if I could sleep in their tent, they'd be welcome to my dope. Though I didn't make it to the festival site that first night, at least I slept well. It turned out to be the only proper sleep I got all weekend.

The next morning, the weather had cleared up and even better, we learnt the festival was now free! I left Montreal with thirty-five dollars and spent a few on the drive down. Since I didn't need to buy a ticket, I was feeling pretty flush. So I made my way over to the liquor store to buy a bottle of something.

That's when I saw this guy with the most amazing coat. It was tan suede and with layers of fringe all the way to the ground. He seemed to shimmer as he walked, like some kind of psychedelic yak. I complimented him on his coat. Smiling, he held out a mint-sized tablet with an American flag on it. "Here you go pal, enjoy yourself!"

I thanked him and dropped the acid expecting to make it to the liquor store and back before it kicked in. But I didn't expect the line-up. When I got finally inside, the shelves were nearly bare and I was very stoned. I ended up getting a jug of cheap Californian fortified wine.

I drifted down a river of people heading the last mile to Yazgar's Farm swigging from the half-gallon jug. It was a beautiful sunny day, and the vibe was nothing but positive. At some point, it occurred to me I wasn't drinking strawberry Kool-Aid. I was guzzling "Gallo Port-Sherry", and I was getting as sloshed as I was stoned.

I woke up in the grass near fence post on the side of the road. I had a sunburn and a parched throat. It was Saturday evening. My first thought was that I had to head back to Bethel to get to a Dairy Queen.

Just then, an "elfin" girl came skipping out of the trees. Of course, I was still lightly tripping and acid has a way putting a Middle-earth spin on things. She asked the most popular question of the weekend, "Where are you from?"

"Canada," I replied.

She asked if I had any Canadian money. I showed her what I had and she judged the coral-coloured bill was the prettiest. She wanted one. I explained this was real money where I came from, and asked if she had a joint she could sell me. She told me to hold on. Minutes later, she returned with a couple joints. I gladly parted with the two-dollar bill.

Thinking some pot was just the thing, I fired one up and proceeded towards town. I hadn't gone far when I looked up and saw a State Trooper leaning against the back of his cruiser. He beckoned me over with his finger. I tossed the joint.

"I'm sorry officer," I sputtered, "no disrespect intended."

He looked me up and down and opened the trunk of the cruiser. He pulled out one of many cartons of Kent cigarettes (likely confiscated contraband), and handed it to me. "Here. You might be able to barter cigarettes for food and water."

At that moment, I considered everything I'd ever heard about the New York State Police might be incorrect. Either that, or I looked much worse than I thought. With the carton of Kents tucked under my arm, I was back on the way to Dairy Queen.

When I got into town, there was a food line along the road that led to some nice ladies from nearby Pennsylvania. They had come to Bethel to provide lemonade and sandwiches for the hungry kids at the Woodstock Festival. I feasted on a ham sandwich and washed it down with lemonade. For dessert, I finally got that ice-milk cone at the Dairy Queen. Refuelled, I was ready to head to Woodstock.

It was 2:30 AM on Sunday when I finally made it to the three-day festival. As I crested a hill, I found myself overlooking the largest crowd I have ever seen. There must have been over three hundred thousand people. On the distant stage was Sly and the Family Stone. I slowly made my way down and through the crowd to a spot that was about 150 feet from the stage. By then, Sly's set was over and The Who's gear was being set up.

The Who did a set of their greatest hits as well as a condensed version of "Tommy." At some point, a guy strode out onto the stage between songs with an unpleasant air of authority.

"Hi everybody, I'm Abbie Hoffman!" he shouted into Peter Townshend's mic. The band clearly had no idea who Abbie Hoffman was, or what he was doing on their stage. He continued, "I think this whole thing is pretty damned irrelevant when John Sinclair is rotting in a Michigan jail."

Pete came up behind Abbie and planted a cross-check with his guitar, sending the famous political activist flying off the stage. The crowd thundered its approval.

By the time The Who wrapped up their show, the sky was starting to lighten. The last scheduled act of Saturday night, Jefferson Airplane, only started playing after dawn on Sunday. Although I was still buzzed from yesterday's acid, watching their ragged-ass jammy set gave me the impression that these guys were more wasted than me. They didn't seem to be having a very good time. I guess that's what happens when your set is delayed by six or seven hours.

After the Airplane wrapped up their set, somebody at the soundboard put a cassette of Jethro Tull's "Stand Up" on repeat. It became the soundtrack for that Sunday morning.

The other piece of music I heard repeatedly at Woodstock was Stevie Wonder's "My Cherie Amour." In 1969, the humble AM transistor radio was still very popular. The station with the clearest signal at Yasgur's Farm was 77-WABC. You couldn't walk two minutes in any direction all weekend without hearing "The Home of the Hits" on somebody's radio. The policy at WABC was to play the #1 Song at the top of each hour. Anytime you heard "My Cherie Amour" it meant a new hour was beginning.

I spent Sunday morning exploring the site. According to Wavy Gravy (Hugh Romney), who was the emcee of the festival, "Woodstock" was now the third-largest city in New York State. According to Mr. Gravy, two people had died by Sunday morning. One was an overdose and the other was someone who had been sleeping in a field and was run over by a joy-rider. On the plus side, two babies had been born and a third was due momentarily.

Behind the stage was a pond where hundreds of people were cooling off in the water. The heat was building all Sunday morning. By the time the first act of the day, Joe Cocker, hit the stage around one p.m., the temperature was at least ninety and the humidity was intense. The next act to come onstage was Country Joe and the Fish. They were only partway through their set when the skies darkened and rain began pouring down. As the storm continued, the hillside turned to mud.

When the rain finally let up, there was the growing rumble of two military helicopters approaching. These enormous khaki-coloured machines had been coming and going all weekend delivering supplies and providing medevac services, but this was the first time two of them were flying side-by-side.

They were soon hovering above the crowd and began dropping what we thought were thousands of white pieces of paper. This was at the height of the Vietnam War and Woodstock had been billed as "Three days of Peace and Music." Like many others, my first thought was the U.S Army might be unloading recruitment leaflets onto this huge anti-war gathering. However, it quickly became clear they weren't leaflets at all; they were thousands upon thousands of white blossoms.

Army helicopters were dropping white flowers on perhaps the largest anti-war gathering ever to have assembled. Meanwhile, Country Joe and the Fish had just led the crowd in a sing-along of "I Feel Like I'm Fixin' to Die Rag", one of the most well-known war protest songs at that time. This couldn't have been more surreal.

To say the rainstorm relieved the heat would be a bit of an understatement. The rain had caused the temperature to drop by about 40 degrees. So now, instead of being a hot and sweaty 90 degrees, it was 50 degrees and everyone was wet and cold. And the sun was setting.

The next act to come onstage was Ten Years After. Actually, they came onstage several times. The temperature was playing havoc with the tuning of the instruments, so the band kept stopping in mid-song and retreating backstage to re-tune.

Though I came to Woodstock hoping to see Jimi Hendrix, he was supposed to close the festival and I didn't think I could made it. By about 8:00 PM Sunday, I was shivering and needed to go home.

I slowly made my way up a muddy slope to the top of the hillside and hopped onto the trunk of a passing car. At the security perimeter, a cop informed us that riding on top of cars was not happening on his shift. I hopped off and continued on foot towards the highway.

Outside the Bethel security perimeter, I met a couple ladies who wanted to know all about Woodstock. They asked if everyone was doing drugs. I said a lot of people were but explained I was really cold and couldn't stand around talking. They offered to drive me back to the New York State Thruway if I would tell them more about the festival.

In the warmth of their car I was happy to answer questions like, "Was there nudity?" ("Until it got cold.") "Was there any free love going on?" ("Here and there.") The ladies weren't disapproving. They were sorry they had missed the party. All too soon, we were at the Northway. I still wasn't dry, but at least I was warmer.

I thanked the ladies and walked out to the highway to hitchhike back to Canada. Luckily, I didn't have to wait more than a few minutes when a black Cadillac pulled over. I opened the front passenger door and was hit by a cloud of marijuana smoke. The driver yelled at the person seated next to him to "get the hell in the back." As I got into the warm, newly-vacated seat, the driver laid down the law, "I need someone to keep me awake. Do you think you can stay awake?"

I assured him I could. He assured me if I couldn't, I'd find my sorry ass on the side of the road. Then he told me to open the glove compartment. There, neatly stacked like a miniature cord of firewood, were dozens of pre-rolled joints.

"Just keep them coming, and don't fall asleep!"

This was something I would normally embrace, but after "Three Days of Peace and Music," it would be a challenge. I took a deep breath and lit the first of many joints. The driver was the self-proclaimed "biggest pot dealer on the south side of Albany." He let me off at a service centre before the state capital and suggested I'd have a better chance of getting a ride at the restaurant than standing at the side of the highway in the middle of the night. He was right.

Almost immediately, I met two guys who were heading to Valleyfield, Quebec. They offered me a ride, though there was no back seat in their Volkswagen Beetle. Turns out there wasn't even a carpet, just a metal floor. But I couldn't be happier with the way my homeward journey was proceeding.

I had smoked so much and was so tired that the next thing I knew, it was morning. And we were on the outskirts of Valleyfield. I didn't even remember waking up for the border crossing, although I suppose I must have. The guys dropped me off at the bus station where I bought a ticket for the forty-minute ride into Montreal.

I had several takeaways from Woodstock. Before the festival, I hadn't realised the magnitude of the counterculture and felt that it might just change our world. I think a lot of the people at Woodstock felt this buzz. Unfortunately, just like an acid trip, new shapes of things tend to gradually reassume their old familiar form. Less than four months after the euphoria of Woodstock, there was the bummer of Altamont. At that concert in California, a young black man was stabbed to death when he pulled a gun on a Hell's Angel who was doing security for the Rolling Stones. Another impression from that weekend was that all my brushes with authority were positive. In 1969, the uniformed people I encountered were reasonable, even sympathetic. The final takeaway was a stubborn chest cold which turned into bronchitis and eventually, pneumonia.

THE FLOYD JONES GROUP

The Floyd Jones Group had reached a modest level of success. By modest, I mean we were booked regularly and each of us might pocket fifteen bucks at the end of a gig.

At the time, if you wanted to hire a rock band in Montreal, everyone knew to call Donald K Donald. And if you did, you'd probably end up talking to a booking agent named Bob Ramaglia. "Rags" would ask your budget and if you didn't have enough for a well-known group, he might sell you "the winner of the Battle of the Bands" for just a bit more than you were willing to pay. Thanks to Rags, we had something of a regular income playing high school dances, frat parties, and community gigs.

One memorable gigs took place in the city of Valleyfield. It was a dance in a community gymnasium. Early in the evening, a motorcycle club showed up. My approach to biker gangs had always been to show respect in the hope they would leave you alone and go away. But they weren't leaving us alone.

One of the leather-clad bikers asked if we knew "House of the Rising Sun." When we said we did, he got up on stage, took the mic and cued us to start playing. Before we knew it, he was belting out the first verse. He wasn't very good but at least he knew most of the words.

When he was finished, the singer took a bow but before we could play the next song, another leather-clad biker hopped on stage, grabbed the mic, and said, "Again." And so we played the song again. When the second biker finished, a third one came on. That night, we ended up playing "House of the Rising Sun" five times. The evening had become a biker sing-off.

The kids in the audience had no idea what to do, which was apparent with the scattered uncertain applause. We also didn't know what to do, so we just kept playing. When the last biker finished, he got off the stage and, without a word, they left.

Our next gig was in a town near the American border called Lacolle. The venue was a banquet hall where they were having a teenage beauty pageant for the next "Mademoiselle Lacolle." About halfway through the gig, one of the organizers, a nice older gentleman, asked us if we could play a processional. Sure, we said. Having repeated the song so many times from the week before, we naturally broke into an instrumental rendition of, "House of the Rising Sun."

Before we knew it, a line of teenage girls started parading across the stage and down the runway. The band and I stifled our amusement as one by one, the maidens of Lacolle strutted their stuff in front of their mothers and aunts while we played an extended version of a song about a New Orleans whorehouse. If the organizers noticed, they didn't seem to care and even gave us a ten-dollar tip.

This one time, we worked a gig at The Mackey Institute for special needs students. During our show, the hearing-impaired kids were up front with their hands on the stage so they could feel the music. We were impressed. Kids who couldn't hear our music could feel it, and they seemed to be liking it. That was until one kid in the middle of the group started signing something.

The kids up front started turning around to see what this kid was going on about. Soon, everyone was ignoring our set and laughing. I think the kid was heckling us. We finished our set a little deflated. But we weren't sure we should feel insulted if our music was not appreciated by people who couldn't hear it.

By far the most memorable gig for the Floyd Jones Group was when we opened for a band called The Deviants. It was a Saturday night at the McGill University Student Union building. There were five acts on the bill. The headliner was a British band called The Deviants. The rest of us were local groups, so the promoter determined the order of appearance by drawing lots. We won, in the sense we'd perform just before the headliner.

The Deviants had a proper dressing room while the rest of us shared a large Green Room. The psychedelic light-show was provided by a group of artists called Pandora's Lights who lived in a commune. They had brought their families to the show and at some point, one of their kids, a boy about ten, walked into the Green Room shaking up a bottle of orange Tang. He was offering refreshments.

I asked to look at the bottom of the bottle. Sure enough, there were about a dozen little purple tabs of what had to be L.S.D. If we drank it, we'd probably be tripping within the hour. Since we still had over an hour before we were due on stage, it seemed like we had to pass. However, I had an idea.

Next up on stage was a band called M.I.C. They were one of those bands that dropped out of the 1968-69 D.K.D. Battle of the Bands because they were too good. They even had a manager, a hyper little man named Jimmy Golightly. I approached Jimmy and suggested their band was too good for us to follow. In reality, they were better players, but our material was straight out of the brain of Stanley Frank, which was pretty incomparable. Jimmy agreed and our two bands switched slots.

I tracked down the acid kid and each of us in the band took one swig. The kid went over to M.I.C., but Jimmy said his band wasn't allowed to drink before a performance. However, there wasn't any reason he couldn't enjoy a tipple. He took a quick swig and said he couldn't taste any vodka. So he took another swig, and then another.

We were just starting to feel the buzz when it was time to perform. We hadn't taken enough L.S.D. to trip, but we were certainly feeling "altered." Luckily, we only had to do a thirty-minute set so we ran through five of our best originals, which we had played countless times, and ended with an acid-driven version of "Time Has Come Today"; a song by the Chambers Brothers. It featured three chords, very few words to remember, and lots of cowbell. Perfect. In fact, Doug Pringle from CHOM thought we killed it and asked if we wanted to do an encore, but we didn't want to push our luck.

Once back in the Green Room, I couldn't find Jimmy anywhere. I only had a small swig and was happily stoned. Jimmy, however, had been chugging the stuff and I was curious how he was getting along. When I finally spotted him, he was sitting cross-legged, rocking back and forth under a grand piano in the corner of the room.

When M.I.C. started playing, Jimmy timidly crawled out. I must have lost track of him because the next thing I knew, he was in the wings dancing wildly. He then bolted on stage, grabbed a mic, and started to sing. One of the band members tried to wrestle the mic out of his hand, but Jimmy wasn't having it. He was going to put on a show.

But he didn't get very far. Whether the guitarist pushed him or simply let go of the mic, Jimmy flew backwards and slammed into the house stack on the side of the stage. The large speaker cabinets toppled down into the crowd. The audience roared. This wasn't even the headliner, and already gear was getting trashed! Luckily, nobody got hurt.

That was it for M.I.C.'s set. The sound company went to work fixing the P.A. and the Deviants were able to take the stage more or less on time. The guys in M.I.C. were pretty upset and were looking for Jimmy, but he had vanished. I spotted him at the end of the night struggling to carry a 70-pound Fender Twin amplifier down a stairwell. I suggested he take the elevator.

"Gotta use the stairs. They told me I gotta use the stairs." There's a chance Jimmy only imagined he was being punished. There's even a chance Jimmy had no idea he was tripping. In those days, it happened.

TAKING THE PLUNGE

Once Laugh-In closed down, I had to get busy completing my last semester at Loyola. Afterwards, I assumed I'd get a job in film-making. However, by the summer of 1971, I was back in Burlington, Ontario working in a lumberyard. I had wanted to check in on my family and ended up sticking around for a while. But after living in Montreal for the last four years, I yearned for the place.

I bought a used Pontiac and one evening when autumn was in the breeze, I decided to drive down to the Burlington Beach Strip where the gasoline was a penny or two cheaper. After filling up, I took the QEW Highway to the Guelph Line, where there were some fast-food restaurants. But instead of turning off, I just kept driving. I hadn't even packed a toothbrush but by the time I passed Toronto, I knew where I was going.

I got to Montreal a little after two in the morning and went straight to the apartment of my old boss Tom Hansen.

Tom and his girlfriend Blanche were still out partying so I waited for them to get back. If the two of them were at all surprised to see me in front of their apartment building unannounced in the middle of the night, they didn't show it. Instead, they invited me in and let me stay until I was set up on my own. I would make one return-trip to Burlington to pick up my things, but I was back in Montreal; this time for good.

Tom was still working as the talent coordinator at "Like Young." By now, the TV show had been renamed "Musical Friends." Since I had a car, I was able to help Tom out with his job. He also helped me find freelance promo work at Polydor Records and some work preparing for the opening of the four-storey Sam the Record Man store on Ste-Catherine Street. I enjoyed my occasional days at Polydor and Sam's, but neither was full-time work.

It took me a couple of months to find my first real position at a company. I had answered a classified ad for a small advertising agency called Consiglio and Associates who were looking for a producer to help them with commercials and film projects who could also do some copywriting.

Advertising in the early 70s really was much like the *Mad Men* TV series. We chain-smoked, drank hard liquor on the job, even in the morning, and for days when we didn't have a hair-of-the-dog, there was an oxygen tank in the office which we would use as a hangover cure. The naked ambition and money-lust was a shock to my liberal arts college/hippie/Laugh-In bartender value system.

I'm not sure I would have lasted long in the advertising business. It's not that I was unsuited to the work; it's just, about once a month I would be involved in a near-fatal accident.

The first time, I was in a car with a Consiglio ad executive who barrelled down a Decarie Expressway on-ramp straight into the side of a semi-trailer. Luckily, we bounced off and into the side wall of the sunken expressway before grinding to a stop.

The next accident was also on the Decarie Expressway. This time the driver was a client, the owner of a company that built truck bodies. We had been in a meeting all afternoon working on a sales catalogue and a bottle of Scotch. That evening, cruising down the expressway in his red Corvette, my client decided to demonstrate a past chapter of his life when he was a race driver. We must have been going about ninety miles an hour in the fast lane when he lost control.

We hit the median wall, skidded across three lanes, slammed into the side wall, flew up the exit ramp to Queen Mary Road, and slowed to a stop at the traffic light. The body of a Corvette was made of fibreglass and much of it was scattered behind us. But we were intact. We were sitting at the red light, seatbelts on, strapped into a sports-car without a body. Remarkably, what was left of the Corvette was working fine so when the light turned green, we continued driving to a party up in Westmount.

A third accident would have been more serious if it hadn't been so cold. The driver was the director of a film we were making for a snowmobile manufacturer and we were on our way to a snowmobile driving lesson. The heater in this Volkswagen Bug didn't work so to keep warm, we were bundled up in all of our snowmobile gear including (...and this is important) helmets.

I should mention the driver was an Englishman who had no experience with winter driving in Canada. Otherwise, he might have realized when the noise of the tires goes quiet, you might be on glare ice. This happened just as we crested a hill at about forty miles an hour on a road which descended and curved towards a bridge over a ravine. If we had any traction, we could have simply slowed down and steered the car. But on an ice-covered gradient, steering can be tricky and braking is a recipe for disaster.

Miraculously, we didn't go into the ravine and instead, slammed into a pillar at one end of the bridge. We hit so hard that my helmet left a dent in the roof of the V.W. Luckily I came out of that with nothing more than a stiff neck.

When we finally went to shoot our Moto-Ski documentary on the Columbia Ice Fields, we had to contend with fast-running rivers, a near-tragedy involving a bottomless crevasse, bear and wolverine encounters, and nighttime lows of minus fifty-five. We also had our entire convoy of ten machines and sleds drive off a thirty-foot cliff, disguised by what's called a "snow bowl."

However, the scariest incident would have been the time I was in a helicopter and it struck a down-draft. One moment we were looking down at the summit of Mount Saskatchewan. The next, we had plunged several thousand feet, stopping just short of slamming into a mountainside. I didn't realize how close we had come to death until I saw the tears in the pilot's eyes.

It was as if I was being warned to get out of the advertising business.

Next to Place Ville Marie in downtown Montreal was a bar called Friday's. I didn't usually spend much time there because I was seldom in that area. But one day after a client meeting, I found myself in the middle of the city, off of work early and enjoying Friday's weekday happy hour. Unexpectedly, I ran into my former employers Donald and Terry.

We started catching up and they asked what I was up to. I explained after getting my degree, I got a job at an advertising agency. Donald was surprised, not because I was working in advertising but that I had a college degree. Neither he nor

Terry had any idea the whole time I was working at Laugh-In, I was also going to university.

Donald, meanwhile, was planning on expanding his concert promotion business. Aquarius Records had a hit. April Wine had released their second album and its first single, "You Could Have Been a Lady," became a Top Five hit in Canada and made the national Top Thirty in America.

At some point during the conversation, Donald casually asked, "So how much money are they paying you at the ad agency?"

"A hundred and fifty," I said.

Donald looked at Terry. He said, "If you want to work for us, we can give you one-twenty-five."

It was quite unexpected and I probably should have taken more time to think about their offer; if for nothing else, to give the semblance of a negotiation. But I was tired of ad people. I was tired of all the bullshit and ad speak. In music, you can either do it or you can't. There's wasn't any faking it, or so I thought. But most of all, I was getting tired of almost dying.

"Sure," I said.

CHAPTER THREE

THE OFFICE

I WAS HIRED TO BECOME a Tour Manager but Donald didn't want to give me a job title or even a job description. He felt it was too limiting. Without a title, he could get me to do anything he needed. I was actually fine with this since I saw an opportunity to learn as much as I could about every aspect of the business.

Also, in early 1972, Donald's tour operation wasn't nearly as busy as it would soon become. As a result, I did a lot of promotional work for Aquarius, helped Bob Lemm with copy for print ads, and found myself in the midst of anything Donald had going on.

MY NEW OFFICE

The original home of Donald K Donald Productions and Aquarius Records was at 180 Dorchester Boulevard, just east of Chinatown. We had two suites facing each other on the second floor of a building that was occupied by accident attorneys and notaries. It was as low rent as a commercial building in that area could be.

There were three owners, Donald, Terry, and Bob, and four distinct businesses, Donald K Donald Productions, Aquarius Records, Terry Flood Management and Promotivation. All net revenue was pooled and split evenly.

The main office always smelled of ether from the mimeograph machine. This contraption was the precursor to the modern photocopier and required someone to hand-crank out multiple copies (or "mimeos") of documents from a stencil. The drying agent in the ink was ether, the same chemical dentists would use to gas unruly kids in the 1950s. Every day in the office, I was reminded of the worst moments of my early childhood.

Every desk had a second-hand intercom which was picked up for cheap at some going-out-of-business sale. The system transmitted nothing but shrieking feedback. The newest technology we had was a fingernail-busting, clattering brute called a telex machine. Thankfully, these contraptions gave way to fax machines.

Off one side of the main room was Terry Flood's office. Terry was the president of Aquarius Records and his Terry Flood Management had two clients, Mashmakhan (which had reformed with Pierre the only original member) and April Wine. His office was usually dimly lit. The furnishings featured lots of dark wood and padded leather and had a faint smell of cigars.

My desk was near the reception and just outside the brightly lit studio where Bob Lemm worked. Bob's company, Promotivation, provided all in-house art services including posters for Donald's shows, packaging designs for all of the Aquarius releases, and print ads for both companies. Bob also had outside clients for the same kind of services.

Across the hall in the other suite were the offices of Donald K Donald Productions, a booking and concert promotion company. Bob "Rags" Ramaglia was D.K.D.'s agent, general manager, and my immediate boss.

When I took a pay cut to work for D.K.D. I didn't realize my $125 ($98 after deductions) would ruffle feathers at the office. It turns out Bob Rags was also earning $125 a week. This was the man who used to get gigs for my band, the Floyd Jones Group. Because I had a college degree and Bob had dropped out of high school, I was no longer the "Floyd Jones kid." I was now "College Boy."

While Rags and I were making the big bucks, everybody else was earning about half that amount including the members of April Wine. But the person most openly upset about this was the office runner, Norman Perry, who was making $55 a week. Norman soon moved to London, England where he found a job working with the top U.K. concert promoter, Harvey Goldsmith, and later returned to Canada to launch one of the most successful rock music merchandise companies in the world, Brockum. He eventually became Donald's west coast production partner.

Although 180 Dorchester East was technically my place of work, I was already starting to spend an increasing amount of time at concert venues.

THE ROLLING STONES BOMBING

The Stones had come to play the Montreal Forum following a Saturday night show in Toronto. Their sound equipment travelled in trucks which arrived on Sunday and were parked on de Maisonneuve Boulevard next to the Forum overnight. Around three a.m. Monday, there was a blast that shook the entire building and blew out windows in nearby apartments. A bomb had exploded.

In recent years, an organization dedicated to an independent Quebec (the F.L.Q.) had detonated explosives around Montreal and the local press speculated the incident might have a political angle. The F.L.Q. was a militant wing of the Quebec independence movement. But it seemed like a spent force by 1972 with many of its leaders in jail or in exile.

It was also suggested the bombing could be payback from the Hell's Angels. The Rolling Stones had been quick to throw the motorcycle club under the bus when the free concert at the Altamont Speedway in California turned deadly. This occurred almost three years earlier and the Angels didn't even have a Montreal chapter in those days. However, The Stones hadn't toured North America since Altamont, so that can't be completely ruled out.

The band's own security people concluded whoever was behind the bombing had a business motive. This seemed like a message targeting the tour, not the general public, since the only loss was financial. Tour organizers had disregarded a warning about using non-union teamsters and blowing up the equipment seemed like just the kind of message they might receive. However, the crime was never solved.

D.K.D. was the promoter. What mattered to us was that the culprit made a mistake. Instead of destroying high-value gear which would be irreplaceable on short notice, the bomb was placed beneath the trailer holding P.A. cabinets. This equipment was not *blown to pieces* as suggested in the news. The shock wave from the explosion merely damaged the cones in the speakers. It was true that unless those speakers could be replaced, the concert would have to be postponed. But this wasn't a hopeless challenge.

Donald and the Stones' road manager, Peter Rudge, got on the phone to source J.B.L. replacement speakers. The only place that had that many was in Los Angeles. And the only way to get them to Montreal on time was to make space in the cargo holds of a flight leaving that day. Donald ended up buying out the entire cargo of an Air Canada flight, hundreds of pounds of rock lobster, to make way for the speakers. That night, an L.A. soup kitchen received a generous donation and served up a feast.

Meanwhile, April Wine's farmhouse just outside the South Shore community of La Prairie was designated as the repair centre. Roadies from several Montreal bands convened at the barn and set to work, opening the cabinets and removing the damaged speakers. By mid-afternoon, the new J.B.L.s arrived at the farm. By five p.m., the Stones' crew was firing up their P.A. system at the Montreal Forum.

However, the bombing wasn't the only problem we were having with the show. There were as many as three thousand counterfeit tickets sold for the Montreal concert and throngs of pissed-off fans were clashing with police in the streets surrounding the venue. It was decided that instead of limousines, the Stones should be transported in less conspicuous vehicles.

Mashmakhan's road manager, Peter Bray, and I went to pick up the band from the Ritz Carlton Hotel in windowless Econoline vans. Limousines were waiting outside, but they would be ferrying members of the band's entourage to the venue. The actual Rolling Stones would be sitting in the back of our vans on overturned milk crates.

Just as planned, our nondescript vans were able to run the gauntlet of protesters and safely deliver our passengers to The Forum without incident. The show started forty-five minutes late because of the bogus tickets, not the bombing.

It seemed like I had already experienced the most memorable part of this exceptional day but for me, the really interesting stuff was just beginning. While the Rolling Stones were busy with their soundcheck, I went for a walk around the backstage area. I passed by the N.H.L. visitors' dressing room and had a peek inside. There, sitting with Donnie Jordan who I knew from the Like Young TV show, was Stevie Wonder!

Stevie was the opening act for the Stones. He was twenty-one at the time and no longer "Little Stevie Wonder", the child prodigy. He had already become one of Motown's best composers and biggest stars. Stevie was, and still is, a hero of mine. And he was sitting *right there*.

Earlier in the spring, I'd bought his latest album, *Music of My Mind,* upon its release. It was my favourite new record of 1972. I worked up the nerve to tell Stevie I loved his music, but nothing prepared me for his new album. I thought this album would win him a lot of rock fans because the new songs were so personal and the production suited the material so perfectly.

I expected he would dismiss me as just one more flatterer. Instead, he replied, "I'm so glad you hear that. If you like this album, I have another one almost finished and two more I'm working on." He had just gone on a songwriting binge. "I don't know what got into me..." he explained.

A few months later, *Talking Book* came out. It had the same kind of animation and intimacy as *Music of My Mind.* I also suspect as early as July of 1972, Stevie Wonder might have had ideas which would make their way onto *Innervisions* and maybe even something which would only be completed for 1974's *Fulfillingness' First Finale.*

Why Stevie Wonder wrote a lot of the best material of his career during one extended rush of creativity happened for reasons I would piece together much later.

My theory goes like this.

When he was "Little Stevie Wonder", Tamla signed him to a recording deal and a publishing deal with Motown's Jobette Music. Any song young Steveland Morris wrote before the age of twenty-one would be published under the original deal. But any song that came along after his twenty-first birthday would be covered by a re-negotiated contract.

Also, the developer of ARP synthesizers, Alan Pearlman, provided Stevie with prototype instruments around 1970. These keyboards could sound like any real instrument or anything you might imagine. They could also store any pass, so they were multi-track recorders. Someone with Stevie's genius would be able to use this new technology to become a one-man Funk Brothers. It's not hard to imagine how these two factors explain the dozens of new song ideas and why Stevie kept many of them under wraps until he was no longer "Little."

The timing of this library of new Stevie Wonder music turned out to be providential. In the summer of 1973, Stevie was involved in a very serious car accident in North Carolina. Initially, it was thought his injury could be career-ending. He spent days in a coma and needed months before he could return to his music. But during this entire period, Stevie Wonder's career continued to go from one height to the next on the strength of a body of work he had put in the bank.

Stevie Wonder checks all the boxes: singer, songwriter, and musician, with all of these skills at the highest level. But then he infuses his work with a positive energy which I can only describe as "love." Meeting Stevie Wonder made this day even more unforgettable.

After the concert, we took the Rolling Stones back to the Ritz Carlton in the old Econolines. Peter Bray and I were asked to stick around in case someone in the band wanted a lift somewhere. It was Ian Stewart's birthday and a party was organized in one of the suites.

I knew Ian Stewart as a roadie who had played some piano on the Stones' early albums. What I didn't realize was Ian was a founding member of the band. Perhaps because he looked more like a Scottish rugby player than a Rolling Stone, he was retired from the stage act in about 1963. But Ian Stewart was still considered a Rolling Stone by the band-members.

Nobody wanted to go for a late-night drive in the back of a van so Pete and I were told we could leave, or we could help ourselves to the beer and stay. Tough decision.

All of the Stones were very friendly except for the new guy, Mick Taylor. He was the guitarist who replaced Brian Jones and who would later be replaced by Ronnie Wood. I later learned that there was a lot of drama between Taylor and the band. That night, it's not that he was unfriendly, he just gave the impression he would sooner be somewhere else.

At about one o'clock in the morning, Mick Jagger showed up. He was greeted by a comment from Keith to the effect, "I thought this was past your bedtime." Mick was chipper and in good spirits, but he didn't stay long. Though he did make sure to raise a glass to Ian.

I mentioned to Charlie Watts how everyone seemed surprised Mick had dropped by. Charlie acknowledged Mick normally didn't hang out with the guys after the show. Tonight was an exception. At about three, "Stewie" headed for the door. This was everyone else's signal to move on as well.

It had been quite a day.

DUMBASS MIKE

Always looking to broaden his business horizons, Donald thought it would be a smart idea to hire a French agent. If it worked, the D.K.D. Agency could expand its artist roster and list of talent buyers. The person recruited to be this agent was a guy named Michel whose last name sounded a lot like the word "niaiseux," which roughly translates to "dumbass." We didn't start off calling him Michel Niaiseux; he earned it.

Michel was a good-looking Quebecois in his early twenties who had the gift of the gab. He could con his way into most situations, especially into ladies' hearts and underwear. Unfortunately, he wasn't as great conning his way out of situations. Also, there was something distinctly "off" about him.

To ease Michel into things, Donald thought it would be a good idea for him to go on a tour with me featuring three Montreal bands; April Wine, a newly re-formed Mashmakhan and Mahogany Rush. The tour would stop in nine smaller Quebec markets which seemed perfect for Michel. Our first task was to advance the shows meaning we would visit venues, ticket outlets, and radio stations and make arrangements for poster distribution.

Our first visit was to a town called Shawinigan. As soon as we were off the island of Montreal, I fired up a small hash joint. I offered it to Michel, but he declined.

"Boy it really smells strong" he commented, rolling down the window.

"Does the smell bother you?"

He said it didn't but kept commenting on how *high* I must be getting. He marvelled that I was still able to drive. I told him I had lots of practice. But he kept mentioning how I might be endangering his life by being so stoned. I figured a simple solution was to let Michel drive.

Though Michel was now behind the wheel, he didn't seem any more comfortable. We were out in the open countryside, yet Michel drove in complete silence with his eyes fixed on the road. At least he stopped complaining.

We were in a region where the two-lane highways feature what are called "Duplessis Curves." Though the land was completely flat for miles in any direction, the highway would suddenly make a series of abrupt right-angle turns. These were created to avoid having to bisect the property of influential farmers who were supporters of politician Maurice Duplessis.

There were warning signs before any curve but when we approached the first one, I noticed we weren't slowing down. "Michel?" I asked.

He didn't seem to hear me. He kept his eyes forward, unblinking and before I knew it, Michel drove us straight off the curve into a farmer's field.

What the fuck, Michel!?

The car wasn't damaged but I decided to relegate Michel to the passenger's seat. I asked him if he hadn't noticed the turn in the road. His response was not reassuring.

"I used to be alright. Before the accident."

Michel explained that a few years ago, he sustained a serious head injury while he was driving a motorboat at his girlfriend's cottage and hit a dock at full speed. It was agreed that from then on, it would be safer if I drove, even if I had a few puffs.

When the actual tour was underway, Michel only got worse. We had an event in Rimouski called Le Festival Western. This cowboy-themed event gave me the impression many people in Rimouski had a fanciful concept of the Wild West. Understandable, since Rimouski is a port on the St. Lawrence Estuary. The people weren't dressed in the cowboy outfits you'd see out West or at the current-day festival in St-Tite in Quebec. These were cowboy (and cowgirl) costumes, the kind you'd see on Halloween or the Roy Rogers TV Show.

The Rimouski concept of the "Western" experience also involved lots of beer. Many people were well into their hops before the sun had set. Several men, women, teens, and even this one German shepherd seemed pretty beery. The spirit was contagious.

The bands wanted to get half-lit before the show just to be in the same space as the audience. I like my beer as well as anyone but decided I really needed to stay sober. My trusty sidekick, Michel Niaiseux, decided the opposite.

Michel was sitting next to me guzzling beer while I was working the door. A young attractive couple walked in with tickets in hand. The guy looked like he was the captain of the local junior hockey team; good-looking, confident, and athletic. His girlfriend was very pretty and otherwise petite, but she wore a tight red sweater over an obviously amble bosom. Michel was drawn to her red sweater like a bull to a matador's cape. As the guy handed over their tickets, Michel suddenly lunged at the girl with a blurry, "Whah." When the guy saw Michel's outstretched hands land on his girlfriend's breasts, in one motion he pulled the tickets away, swung around and slammed his fist into Michel's head.

He punched Michel so hard he flew off his stool and landed on the floor, about five feet away. I apologized to the couple but the sight of Michel knocked unconscious on the floor lying next to his snot, eased any tension. He handed over their tickets again, and they went in to enjoy the show. Michel was helped off to one of the bands' dressing rooms, where he would remain for the rest of the evening.

After the show, we headed further down-river to a town called Matane-sur-Mer so we could make the first ferry across the St. Lawrence the next morning, otherwise we'd late arriving in Sept Isles. I was driving with Michel and the three members of Mahogany Rush and at some point, one of them said, "I don't suppose there's any place out here where we could get some food?"

We pulled into a roadside diner on the outskirts of nowhere and the other cars in our little convoy followed. I woke up a snoring Michel, but he wanted to stay in the car. He claimed he was coming down with the flu and didn't want to eat anything in case it made him sick. The rest of us went in and enjoyed a late supper.

When we returned to the car, the passenger door was open and Michel was gone. I wasn't fazed. "It looks like Michel has decided to walk home," I joked.

Someone asked if we should double-back towards Rimouski to look for him. I thought there was no need. If Michelle decided to head back the way we came, it's likely he took off in the wrong direction and was heading the same way we were going. So we piled into the cars and continued our journey to Matane. Within about half a mile we spotted Michel staggering along the side of the road.

We woke up early the next morning and caught the first ferry. Michel was hungover and no doubt still feeling the effects of being knocked out the night before. He laid down on a bench and placed a piece of cardboard next to him. On it, he had written in French, "I'm a musician who works at night. Please don't wake me." When Michel had passed out, Pierre from Mashmakhan took the sign, flipped it over and wrote (also in French), "I'm a gay prostitute. Only wake me if you have cash."

The last show of our little tour we in a baseball field in Alma and drew over 4,000 concert-goers. We decided when the show was over, we would all help with the load-out and drive the seven hours back to Montreal. Some friends of Mahogany Rush had driven up from Montreal to give them a lift home, so it was just me and Michel in the rented car.

The first half of the trip took us through the vast La Verendrye Park. By the time we passed Quebec City and were back on The Trans-Canada Highway, it was daylight. Michel had been asleep up to this point. Now he became his usual annoying self.

"I can't believe you're still awake. I'm scared you're gonna fall asleep and crash the car. How can you still be awake?" This went on for several miles but I guess my judgement was impaired; I pulled off onto the shoulder and let him drive.

Michel drove at slightly less than sixty miles an hour while the rest of the traffic seemed to be going at least eighty. I suggested he had to speed up a little but he started mumbling "I'm going too fast, I'm going too fast," over and over. At the same time, he was slowing down.

By now, semi-trailers were thundering past us. I started to panic. "Pull over!" I yelled. Finally, when we hit about twenty miles an hour on what was then one of the fastest stretches of highway in the country, Michel said, "Oh no, the curtain is coming down. It's coming down, can't you see it? The birds are coming, the birds are coming…"

I grabbed the steering wheel with one hand and threw the car into neutral with the other. Once on the shoulder, we coasted safely to a stop. Michel was still carrying on about the curtain coming down and the attack of the birds. I don't know what a doctor would make of his mental state. Maybe this was a result of his boating accident, or maybe this had been the cause.

After our tour of Quebec, Michel found himself without a place to stay and began sleeping at the office. One morning, the three women on the staff were waiting downstairs in the lobby. Apparently, for the past few days, the first person who arrived would find Michel sleeping nude on the bench in the main office. And being a young man in his early twenties, let's just say, the mornings could be hard.

Even before the tour, I felt Michel had issues and expressed my concerns to Donald and Rags. I tried to explain that he wouldn't be able to help the agency succeed in the French-language market. But what finally convinced them was Michel Niaiseux sleeping naked with an erection at our reception.

I never knew whether or not to feel sorry for "Dumbass Mike." On one hand, mental disability is a serious issue and nothing to laugh at. On the other, I had to put up with him. The last time I saw Michel was on a 105 Sherbrooke Street bus. He was with a young, pretty woman and waved to me as I got off. All I could think was how good it was that he wasn't driving.

COMPETING WITH THE FORUM

Even without the help of a French-speaking agent, Donald's business expanded. Aquarius had just received its first gold album, April Wine's *On Record*, and the concert business was exploding. There was a time when the top concert promoter in Montreal was Sam Gesser. The story goes that Donald and Sam co-promoted a show starring Janis Joplin where, at the end of the night, Janis vomited on Sam's shoes. That's when Sam decided to get out of the rock business.

Donald learned early on, after losing money with Forum shows starring artists like R&B singer Joe Tex or Country Music icon Hank Snow, the safest plays were rock bands. Meanwhile, the people at the Montreal Forum were impressed Donald paid his bills even when his show lost money. They decided by the late sixties that he would be their exclusive rock concert promoter. Never again would Donald have any problem contacting agents. The top agents would reach out to him because Montreal was one of the top forty concert markets in North America. Plus, an N.H.L. arena (like the Forum) was considered a prime venue.

However, The Forum management saw how much money Donald was making and decided to double the rental rate. Then they doubled it again, but he was still making money. Finally, The Forum decided they would become concert promoters themselves. Donald K Donald Productions would now be limited to a fee for booking, marketing and managing the shows. He could still earn a bonus if sales were good enough, but Donald's first reaction was to rebel.

He decided to find a new venue in Montreal as an alternative to the Forum. He picked a place in the suburbs called the Pierrefonds Arena which might hold 3000 people, a bit less than the 18,000 concert capacity of The Forum. The shows would be branded "Donald K Donald and Al Gregory Presents…" so Donald could tell The Forum that he wasn't in competition; he was just showing the ropes to an old friend. In reality, Al Gregory was the contractor who provided security teams for The Forum shows.

Donald booked two "can't fail" packages. In each case, a British star attraction was supported by a new American band. In both cases, the support act stole the show.

The first concert starred Procol Harum; a very good band with some great songs. But their opening act was something else. I was walking by their dressing room as they were rehearsing vocal harmonies. I stuck my head in the door and asked if I could listen. They waved me in. As I sat there, I couldn't believe how perfect it sounded. All I knew about this band was that they had some involvement with Linda Ronstadt and they had this one single, "Take it Easy." This was the first time I'd seen or heard Eagles.

The second concert was about six weeks later. The headliners were T-Rex and they drew a larger, livelier crowd.

But their performance faltered. The popular image of Marc Bolan was this waifish, poetic, glam-rock icon. But the guy on stage that night was a little hefty and a lot drunk. Even the great T-Rex repertoire couldn't save the show. Meanwhile, the opening act was on a mission to kick ass. They were The Doobie Brothers.

Even if Donald could make money doing shows in Pierrefonds, the idea of booking A-List talent into a hockey rink in the suburbs wasn't going to work for very long. Those were the only two shows "Donald K. Donald and Al Gregory Presents…" ever put on. Donald had to accept his new status as the "hired promoter" at The Forum. However, if a major artist wanted to route a tour through Montreal, Donald would try to convince them to also play The Civic Centre in Ottawa and Le Colisée in Quebec City, where he could still be the promoter and rent the arenas for a flat fee.

CHAPTER FOUR

ON THE ROAD

MARK TWAIN FAMOUSLY CLAIMED THAT "travel is fatal to
bigotry." I would add, "unless you're in a car." The million-
plus miles I spent behind the wheel in those days may have
made me more bigoted, especially towards Winnebagos
driving 40-mph on two-lane highways. But once I got out
of the car, I found that people all across the country were
friendly, helpful and seldom in my way.

Another thing I found is that if you're up for adventure,
you have to be ready for the occasional misadventure. A lot of
the time, it's better to be lucky than smart. It's remarkable that
things worked out as well as they did, though I attribute a
lot of my luck to the fact I was in Canada. Looking back, the
most profoundly memorable aspect of those years wasn't any
one show or specific incident; it was experiencing Canada.

OH, CANADA

We were promoting Canadian bands on regional tours so the
obvious next step was to link the regions and form a national
circuit. I got to play an instrumental role in helping Donald

K Donald develop this circuit that ran from Newfoundland to Vancouver Island.

Before any tour, Donald and the band's manager would agree on the timeframe, budgets and support acts. After that, I would go to work. I looked after media buys at radio, newspapers, and television, and rented most of the arenas and halls. Then I'd need to arrange for things like staging, stagehands, electrical requirements, security, advance sales and box office/ door staff. But in terms of planning, the most important part of the job was to route the dates, making sure all the jumps were realistic.

The obvious factor was travel-time and hitting the right markets on the right days. We always wanted to play Fridays and Saturdays in the biggest cities and to hit everything else in between. When we did have a day off, it usually involved serious mileage. Since I did a number of tours with different acts each year and often advanced those tours, in a given season I might drive 250,000 miles.

During the winter months, driving in Canada can actually be dangerous. Crossing British Columbia, you encounter one mountain range after another. The prairies can get so cold that salt has no effect on ice and even busy roads like the Trans-Canada Highway can be treacherous.

As a result, my work was seasonal. But it could be a long season. I usually hit the road in March and called it a year by November. The latest I ever got caught in a snowstorm was June 5th near Timmins, Ontario and the same year, I encountered blizzard conditions in September just after Labour Day near Radium Hot Springs, B.C. As the Canadian joke goes, that's nine months of winter and three months of poor skating conditions.

The crew's schedule dictated what routing was possible. Say the crew wanted to start load-in at two pm and the load-out should be finished by midnight. A normal day involved ten hours at the venue, six hours for sleeping, and eight hours for everything else (including travel). I soon knew the distances, the roads, and even the traffic conditions we could expect travelling coast-to-coast.

The trip from North Sydney, Nova Scotia, to Port aux Basques, Newfoundland, was usually between eight to nine hours on the water. If there were icebergs it would take longer and the seas could be rough. After landing at Port aux Basques in Newfoundland, there were still a couple of hours drive to the nearest city (Cornerbrook). A full day was always set aside for travelling to and from "The Rock."

Newfoundland only joined Canada at the start of July 1949. "The Rock" always had, and probably always will have, its own culture. There are villages that were established by Basque and Portuguese fishermen before Columbus ever set sail. A Newfoundland accent is as distinct as any you'll find in Ireland or Scotland. Some settlements can still only be reached by boat. They have their own half-hour time zone. Newfoundlanders, or "Newfies" as they're affectionately known, have their own way of doing things.

In Cornerbrook, the local dealers would only sell us nickels of pot in small matchboxes claiming the Horsemen, meaning the RCMP, "leave you alone if you only have a nickel." Marystown, at the tip of a long peninsula, had winds so strong, all the tree trunks were curved and the phone lines had to be strung on tripods. In Gander, the crew supper was moose-steaks. Harbour Grace was the only place where I arrived at an arena to find the manager smoking pot with the rink rats.

In St. John's, I was going for an interview with the Stampeders at the TV station and got lost. There was a cop parked at the side of the road so I asked for directions. The conversation went something like this:

"Excuse me, sir, do you know how to get the TV station?"

"So, you're lookin' for the TV station?"

"Yes."

"Jeez boy, I don't think you can get from here to there."

"That's odd, I thought you could get there from here."

"Oh, *for me* that's not a problem."

I had no idea where this was going. But then he continued, "Wait a minute! Why don't you follow me?"

Another time, we were at a motel/restaurant on the highway separating Windsor and Grand Falls and had what may have been the most "only on The Rock" experience. The coffee shop doubled as a cowboy-themed saloon, so it had the kind of swinging louvered doors you see in Western movies. I was sitting at the bar eating breakfast when a large female skunk came waddling out of the rear hallway, through the dining area, and out under the front door. The whole room immediately reeked. I quickly made my way with the other diners to the large veranda to get some fresh air.

I said to a waitress, "I always heard there weren't any skunks here in Newfoundland."

"That's true, not in the wild. But she's pet skunk," she replied.

I asked, "When you have a pet skunk, shouldn't you have it de-scented?"

"Maybe on the mainland. But when it's the only skunk on the whole island, you don't want to ruin her, do you?"

Just then, a Volkswagen Beetle that doubled as a duck blind sped past us on the Trans-Canada Highway leaving a trail of dried reeds in its wake. This certainly wasn't the mainland.

The other Atlantic Provinces were just as memorable, but for very different reasons. The most scenic of these was probably Nova Scotia. The Cabot Trail traces the rugged coastline of Cape Breton and some stretches of the Trans-Canada Highway make it an accessible wonder. But practically any part of Cape Breton makes you want to stop the car and take a picture.

Peggy's Cove has a lovely little lighthouse on a pretty out-cropping of tide-worn rock, but if I was taking a day-trip out of the vibrant mini-metropolis of Halifax, I'd want to visit the Three Sisters at the head of the Bay of Fundy near Kentville. Here's a case where tides have created rock formations that resemble the crayon drawings of an imaginative six-year-old.

In July 1972, I watched a total solar eclipse at Prince Edward Island's Stanhope Beach as camera crews from Life Magazine and National Geographic were set up on the sand dunes behind me. Visiting Prince Edward Island in those days entailed a boat ride and from the water, the gently rolling topography looked landscaped.

I found New Brunswick's most publicized attractions to be underwhelming. Saint John's Reversing Falls is a small water-fall at low tide and at high tide, the current flows upstream. In the seventies, if you wanted to spend the time it takes to witness this slow-motion phenomenon, your eyes would be burning from the acrid air pollution of a nearby Irving pulp mill. Moncton's Tidal Bore is boring. There was a time when an impressive wave would storm up the Petitcodiac River twice a day at high tide. But the province dammed the river so now it's just a vast mudflat that slowly fills with water.

The places in New Brunswick which really do deliver the goods include the beautiful coastline and 19th-century charm of St. Andrew's-by-the-Sea, Canada's warmest salt-water beaches at Shediac, or the dramatic mountains at the head of the Bay of Chaleur where Quebec's Gaspé Peninsula meets New Brunswick.

The mouth of the Saguenay River in Quebec is spectacular, as is Sleeping Giant Island near Thunder Bay in Ontario. There's even this place called Niagara Falls. But I'd say the real attractions of Canada's two largest provinces are Canada's two largest cities, Montreal and Toronto, as well as the capitals of the two Canada's, Quebec City and Ottawa.

Further west is the Canadian Shield and the Prairies. These huge sections of Canada are what I might call acquired tastes. Before you get to the Prairies, there's a "shortcut" across the massive Canadian Shield on the Trans-Canada Highway, which only takes about twenty hours. This unbroken stretch of rocks and trees and lakes is the essence of Eastern Canada.

Then there's The Prairies. For fifteen hundred miles the most dramatic thing you'll see on a given day might be the sky. But I wouldn't say there isn't anything to see. The original settlers' wagons were called Prairie Schooners probably because the middle of Canada is like a gently rolling ocean of grassland where the sky is vast and often beautiful.

Once in a while, there will be a valley that's all the more remarkable after hundreds of miles of plains. The most spectacular of these is the aptly-named Big Valley. The first time I descended into the verdant valley near the "dinosaur capital of the world", Drumheller, I was coming from the Saskatchewan side. The transition was so dramatic it felt like I'd fallen through a time portal into an epoch before humans existed. I could easily imagine this was where dinosaurs once roamed.

But any trip across Canada from East to West reserves the best for last.

Driving Highway 93 from Banff to Jasper in the shadow of the towering peaks of the Canadian Rockies is awe-inspiring. I wouldn't mind making that pilgrimage every couple of years. But for the ultimate alpine experience, take the twelve-hour drive from Calgary to Vancouver on the Trans-Canada Highway.

Travelling from the Alberta foothills to the waters of the Pacific, you encounter five major mountain systems. And the monster isn't the Rockies which borders Alberta or the Coastal Range you see in Vancouver. It's the astounding Columbia Mountains which are the true backbone of British Columbia; notably the Selkirk Range. How the first explorers found their way through this barrier is mind-boggling. Even at the height of summer, it's evident how unforgiving this environment is.

By the time you finally reach the Pacific you have to be impressed by the remarkable country you have traversed. Yet there's one last wonder to experience; Vancouver Island. If America has Hawaii, Canada's island paradise is Vancouver Island with its warm (for Canada) weather, spectacular scenery, and mellow vibe. The first time my touring brought me here I had a strong impulse to stay. After Montreal, it's my second favourite Canadian island.

In the seventies, I travelled enough miles to circle the globe at least fifty times but aside from day-trips to Vermont and New York, I never left Canada. Those years of touring underlined what an amazing place Canada is. The great George Carlin pointed out that being proud of where you were lucky enough to be born is just plain dumb. So rather than proclaim I'm proud to be Canadian, I'll just say I can't believe my luck.

THE MUSHROOM FERRY

During my touring days, there was one undisputed travel highlight. It was a ferry route I only ever took with The Stampeders that took about twenty-one hours and would sail between Campbell River on Vancouver Island and Prince Rupert (which is about forty miles from the Alaskan Panhandle). We would rent cabins on board the ferry boat, buy food and enjoy the kind of sights the cruise ship companies advertise. The one-way trip used to cost about twenty dollars per person and fifty for cars.

I had a very dear friend named Cindy who belonged to the Tseshaht tribe based at the head of the Alberni Inlet. Whenever The Stampeders played Port Alberni, the Tseshalt were welcome to come to the show. They reciprocated by providing us with magic mushrooms. Once they even took us into the cow pastures where the "shrooms" grew in old dried up cow pies. We would always get enough mushrooms for the entire entourage to get high for the day on the ferry.

Magic mushrooms are like L.S.D.'s organic and mild-mannered cousin. The psychedelic trips did not involve the chaos of "peaking", they didn't last as long, and I never experienced any after-effects. There might have been some visual aberration, a body high, and a feeling of euphoria, but what I always experienced while high on mushrooms was a sense of being at one with my surroundings. In nature, and especially in a place where nature is so spectacular, the mushrooms can truly seem magical.

The strait between Vancouver Island and the mainland where the ferry departs Campbell River is quite wide. But travelling north, the strait narrows. Sometimes we'd see deer or the occasional moose looking back at us from the shores.

The mountains on the island are lower than the mainland so on a sunny late afternoon, the light would gleam through gaps in the island hills and flood the side of the mountains on the mainland. Distant waterfalls would glisten like shiny strands of tinsel.

Sometimes a pod of dolphins would keep pace with the ferry for a stretch and it wasn't unusual to see a herd of seals splashing along the water's edge. Ospreys floated on the updrafts seeking schools of fish to dive-bomb.

When the boat cleared the strait, we'd be in the open Pacific for several hours. In contrast to the serene protected waters of Vancouver Island Sound, the open Pacific would usually have some very large waves. The waves from the north would battle the waves from the west with the boat caught in the middle. Often, the boat would end up in this sort of "figure-eight" wobble. And the higher the waves, the wilder the wobble.

On one particular trip, the blues skies and bright sunlight of our passage through the sound had given way to steely grey clouds in the open sea. We were well into our shrooms and the car deck near water level was a great place to feel at one with the power of the ocean. The boat felt like it was being swallowed and spat out with every wave as the wind whipped at our hair and sprayed saltwater across the deck. Being down there aroused a deep and almost dark sense of awe. But for everyone else on the boat who wasn't on mushrooms, it evoked nausea. The queues for the toilets were so long we found a new use for the Dixie cups in our dressing room supplies.

The final phase of the trip was after daybreak in the relative calm of the Queen Charlotte Islands Sound. By now, the mushrooms would be waning so we would spend the rest of our little voyage eating, laughing, drinking, and snoozing. It was always the perfect ending to the perfect travel day.

CHURCHBRIDGE SK

One year we somehow managed to book fourteen shows for The Stampeders in Saskatchewan and two just over the border in Russell and Dauphin, Manitoba. We had played Saskatoon on a Saturday night and we were headed for the show in Russell on Sunday when I was involved in a bizarre accident.

A local promoter named Dave Warren helped organize the set of dates but was too busy to actually work the tour so he'd hired a guy from Toronto named Bob to be our day-to-day local contact. I probably had more experience working the arenas of Saskatchewan than anyone from Toronto unless they were a hockey scout. And I liked Saskatchewan; Bob didn't.

Bob was driving and on the open stretches of the two-lane highways where the posted limit was fifty miles per hour, he had trouble keeping it under eighty. In those days, they had grain elevators every ten miles along the rail lines which usually paralleled the highways. The land was so flat that after passing one elevator, you could see the next one off in the distance.

There was a small dust cloud along the horizon in the field to the left of the highway. A minute passed and the cloud seemed to be getting bigger. I remarked that it seemed to be approaching the highway at a right angle. A minute later, I was pretty sure the dust was being kicked-up from a fast-moving vehicle closing-in on the highway. Another thirty seconds passed and I offered the opinion that whatever was speeding through the field might intersect with us.

"Not my problem," said Bob. He explained, 'We're on the highway. We have the right of way.'

This was true but potentially irrelevant. Soon, I could make out a yellow pickup truck bounding through the fields going almost as fast as we were.

"Bob, I think you'd better slow down," I suggested.

"I think *he'd* better slow down", he corrected.

In the movie *Monty Python and the Holy Grail,* there is a scene where Sir Lancelot attacks a castle. Guards at the gate are letting peasants through and notice someone off in the distance. We hear a drumroll as the camera cuts to Lancelot at the far end of a field running towards them. We cut back to the guards casually watching. Cut back to the drumroll and Lancelot back at the far end of the field running. We cut back to the guards, one of them now eating an apple. Cut back to Lancelot back at the far end of the field. They cut to the same clip of Lancelot running four times! Suddenly, Sir Lancelot jumps into frame and stabs a guard without the other even noticing. This whole scene takes 43 seconds and is nowhere near as ridiculous as what happened to us.

I had watched this truck coming towards us at full speed for three whole minutes and then suddenly, Bam! It slammed into us. The back of our station wagon was t-boned. Hard. It didn't just feel like it was slow motion. It actually was.

Our car was tossed into the air and we spun around. The back of our wagon clipped a telephone pole before we slammed down sideways into a muddy ditch.

The windows were blown out and a lot of beer, which we were carrying for dressing room supplies, popped. I figured I was still alive because I didn't think the afterlife smelled like beer. Somehow, the radio was still playing "Strawberry Letter 23."

"Bob… you okay?" I asked.

We were mired in the mud at roughly a 45-degree angle with the driver-side wheels in the air. Neither Bob nor I were hurt and we managed to climb out of his side and out of the ditch.

We saw that the back half of our Chevy wagon was crushed. We looked over at the telephone pole and saw a chunk was missing.

Sitting in the middle of the road was the yellow pickup truck with its mangled cab bent like an L-shape at right angles to its box. Its driver didn't appear to be injured and was staggering around the road.

"I guess I should have stayed in the field and slept this one-off'", he suggested, eliminating any doubt he was drunk.

The first person at the scene was a lady who lived in the house nearby. She asked if everyone was OK before turning her attention to the wreck. Hands-on hips, she pronounced, "That's what's wrong with these new cars; they're so nice in the showroom but if you get one tiny scratch, they look like shit." She looked over at the pole and said, "Too bad you guys didn't knock down that God-damned eyesore."

We didn't know what to say so she continued, "You mind if I syphon off the gas before it leaks into the ditch? After all, it doesn't look like you're goin' anywhere in this car."

I assured the astute woman that she was welcome to the gasoline. In fact, she was welcome to the whole car.

We started unloading our bags and whatever backstage supplies we could salvage. By now, a crowd from the nearby town of Churchbridge had started to gather and a police car arrived. Two officers approached us. Their uniforms looked exactly like RCMP-issue; distinctive bluish-grey shirt and deep blue pants with broad yellow stripes down the side. Except the shoulder patches read, "Churchbridge Constabulary." And they seemed a bit short and hefty to be Mounties.

The one with a couple of stripes sewn onto the arms of his shirt was clearly in charge. He asked, "So what are you two doing in Churchbridge on a Sunday morning with all this beer?"

I told him we were promoters for a Stampeders' show down the road in Russell. He looked us up and down and seemed satisfied. He then turned his attention to the two wrecked vehicles. "Well, it looks like no one is to blame. Clearly, it's just an accident, and *accidents will happen.*"

I was incredulous.

"What you mean? The joker who plowed into us is *drunk as a skunk*, check him out. Not to mention, he comes barreling out of a fucking field and smashes into us as we're driving down the highway. No one to blame? Holy shit, we could have been killed!"

The cop then tells me I should mind my language since there were women and children present, indicating the onlookers. Just then, a cooler head prevailed. He was a tall, blond kid about eighteen years old. He took me by the arm and led me away from the cop.

In a calm voice, he explained, "Nobody's going to charge the other driver. He works for my father."

"What is that supposed to mean?" I asked.

"Well", he continued, "the field he drove out of belongs to my father. And so do the fields on the other side of the highway. In fact, the town over there," he pointed at Churchbridge, "A lot of it belongs to Dad too."

"Including Tweedle Dee and Tweedle Dum," I suggested, nodding towards the two cops.

"Pretty well," said the young man.

I quickly realized nobody was going to do anything about the accident. I decided to ditch our trashed rental and get out of there. We had a show to put on. "Can your dad also take care of this wreck?" I asked.

"I'll take care of it myself," he said.

I asked him how far it was to Russell. "About a ten-hour walk," he says and then smiles, "But I'll give you a lift."

"No need," I said. "In a few minutes, a big truck and smaller truck will come down the highway and take us where we're going."

He explained that hardly anyone would come down this road on a Sunday morning unless they're headed to church. Just then, the Stampeders' five-ton truck appeared on the horizon followed by the support band's van.

Ten minutes later I was watching Churchbridge receding in the rear-view mirror.

BETWEEN TOURS WITH A BAG FULL OF CASH

One of my earliest tours swung through Western Canada, taking me west with Lighthouse and then back east with Crowbar. I remember it mostly for the transition day.

Lighthouse had played Penticton, the most southerly city in the Okanagan Valley, on a Friday night. The next show was in Victoria, on Vancouver Island, the next day. To get there, Lighthouse, their crew, and I would have to drive over 200 miles to the coast through the Coastal Mountain Range, and encounter the notoriously unpredictable wait times for the Tsawwassen ferry. After an hour and a half on the water, we'd still have a forty-five-minute drive on Vancouver Island. If everything went perfectly, the entire trip would take almost seven hours but we would budget for nine.

When we arrived in Victoria, there was plenty of time to set up the band and the opening act. Most stops had different opening acts and for the final date, we had a Canadian magician named Doug Henning. In the next couple of years, he would become an international star; his signature moustache and mullet a fixture on American television. But on that night, he was just a magician at a rock concert.

The show drew a crowd of over 3,000 which was a perfect way to cap-off the Lighthouse tour. The next morning, I was to get back to Vancouver, hop on a flight to Saskatoon, and begin touring with Crowbar. However, my schedule had been so packed that I didn't have a chance to get to a bank all week. I was carrying the cash profits from show to show and by the time I left the Victoria Memorial Gardens, I had $12,000 (about $75k in today's money) in one, two and five-dollar bills stuffed in a bag.

Our co-promoter in British Columbia was Bruce Davidson and I worked the B.C. portion of the tour with his assistant Terry. We were planning on travelling back to Vancouver together the next morning. Because of the tight schedule from Penticton, we only were able to check in to the motel after the Victoria show.

It was past midnight so the night manager was on duty. We had guaranteed reservations and he was ready for us until Terry asked, "Oh, do you guys have a safe? We have a lot of money and I would sleep better knowing it wasn't in our room."

I couldn't believe what I was hearing. A big part of my security strategy relied on the fact I looked like someone who wasn't carrying more than forty bucks. But now, we looked like a pair of drifters who may or may not have stolen a bagful of cash.

I told Terry that before handing over the money, we would have to count it all, get a receipt, and then recount when we got it back in the morning. I would sleep better if we didn't have to do all that. Terry agreed, but now the night manager looked concerned.

Early the next morning, we loaded up the rental car and left. But just as we got to the end of the parking lot, R.C.M.P. cars screeched to a stop in front of us with lights flashing. They had blocked as in and came at us, guns drawn. They even had a dog.

Fortunately, we didn't get shot or bitten but by the time I convinced the police I could account for all the cash, I was certain to miss my flight.

I managed to catch the next flight out to Saskatoon and landed sometime in the late afternoon. I then went to rent a car counter. I was under twenty-five at that time. I knew this could be an issue so I made sure to get a letter from the head office of Budget authorizing their franchisees to waive the age requirement. However, when I got to the Budget counter in Saskatoon, I was told it didn't matter what the letter said; they weren't renting me a car. Why not? Because my credit card didn't have a high enough limit in the event I never brought the car back.

Now I was getting pissed off.

First, I missed my flight because the motel night-manager in Victoria didn't believe a hippie could be carrying a lot of money legitimately. Now, I was going to miss the show because this guy didn't believe a hippie could have *enough* money.

"How much is your Chevrolet worth?" I asked.

I opened the bag and began pulling out bundles of cash, slapping them on the counter.

"What if I give you a $4000 deposit? Here, make it five…"

That's when, for the second time on the same day, I ended up talking to the R.C.M.P.

Again I showed my settlement sheets and piles of receipts. I explained what had happened earlier in the day, and why I was in a rush to get to North Battleford. Luckily, the police were sympathetic and helped me to rent a car from Avis, without leaving a deposit.

By the time I finally got out onto the open prairie, the sun was setting on the Yellowhead Highway. I felt strangely calm, considering I was at least five hours behind schedule and had no idea what was awaiting me in North Battleford. This was the first time I felt the tranquil beauty of the prairies.

When I got to the arena, the opening act was already on stage, the audience was in good spirits, and the arena manager and my local contact had everything under control. I couldn't believe it. Things were finally going right. I went to the band's dressing room to apologize and explain my lateness.

When I introduced myself as the promoter, Crowbar's leader Kelly Jay said, "Thanks for stopping by. Will you be staying for the show?"

After I recounted the story of my journey from Vancouver Island, he assured me, "Shit happens, brother, but you're safe now. You could probably use a beer and something to smoke." I doubt Kelly remembered me from Laugh-In, but he treated me like an old friend.

CHAPTER FIVE

THE STAMPEDERS

A LARGE PART OF THIS book deals with two bands; The
Stampeders and April Wine. Both bands are still remembered
today, although neither was ever considered the top rock
band in Canada at any given point. However, in the 1970s
these two groups probably played more headline concerts
in Canada than any of their contemporaries. And at least up
until 1978, The Stampeders was the busier of the two bands.

I had my first encounter with the Stampeders at the Maple
Music Junket show in Montreal in June 1972. Soon afterwards, Donald and the band's manager, Mel Shaw, agreed
to do a winter tour of Eastern and Northern Ontario. This
would be the first of many shows I would work with the
Stampeders. Later, the band pioneered Donald K Donald's
national circuit and I crossed the country with them on six
different tours. Between 1972 and 1977, I managed well over
400 of their concerts.

These are some of the stories from those tours.

THE BAND

The Stampeders are most famous for their three-man formation consisting of bassist Ronnie King (real name Cornelius Van Sprang), drummer Kim Berly (real name Kimberly Meyer), and guitarist Richard Dodson (his real name). However, the original Stampeders also included Kim's older brother, Race, Ronnie's older brother, Vann, and Brendan Lyttle. This six-man group started in Calgary before moving to Toronto. To set up shop in the East, they needed to get approval from the American Federation of Musicians.

At the time, the executive of Local #149 in Toronto included some doo-wop Brylcreem-slicked cats who didn't want more long-haired rockers tainting their art; especially bands from "out west." But the Stampeders needed the transfer if they hoped to tap into Canada's most lucrative market. So they came to a compromise.

The Stampeders would need to live in Toronto and start paying their dues, but they couldn't play anywhere near Toronto for the first two years. The Stampeders would be making drives to places like Ottawa, London, Sudbury, and Montreal just to pay the rent. The long hours of travel for small rewards soon took a toll and the three older members packed it in and headed back West. The remaining Stampeders stuck with it, put in their 10,000 hours playing together, and scored a remarkable international hit with "Sweet City Woman."

By 1972, The Stampeders were a tight little operation. They had a two-man crew on the first shows I did with them. Bob "Luffy" Luffman was the soundman and Joel Wickhammer was the light-man/electrician. Soon afterwards, they added Ian "Snake" Dunbar to be the stage tech and monitor mixer.

Because the Stampeders had worked together for years and knew their roles in the arrangements, the band was naturally "tight." They hardly ever did soundchecks. The crew would do a line-check, checking all the electrical connections, and when the band took the stage, they used the first song for a soundcheck. With Luffy on the board, things usually sounded fine by the first chorus of the first song.

They could play on a wrestling ring, loading-in at five p.m. and doors open at seven. With a ticket price of two dollars (two-fifty at the door), as long as five hundred kids showed up, they would make a profit. Of course, ticket prices increased every year and the shows drew between seven hundred to three thousand customers. We made good money.

All three musicians sang and wrote songs, but Richard had an edge in both departments. His song "Sweet City Woman", is an example of his exceptional talent, but he also wrote and arranged "Carry Me", "Wild Eyes", "Devil You", and about a dozen other recognizable songs.

Richard also had the best vocal pitch of the three and usually, the most complex aspect of any Stampeders' song was his guitar work. He hand-made his famous double-neck Gibson by sawing and gluing together a twelve-string and a six-string. His playing was precise, structured, and hardly varied from year-to-year, let alone night-to-night. But Richard couldn't connect with audiences the way Kim and Ronnie could. Richard was imaginative yet methodical, while Ronnie and Kim were all about feeling and vibe.

Kim's biggest hits were country favoured songs like "Oh My Lady" and "Minstrel Gypsy." He also sang some of Richard's best-known compositions like "Devil You" as well as covers like "Hit the Road Jack", "New Orleans" and "Memphis, Tennessee" which often challenged the top of his range. From my perspective, Kim was always ready to do whatever was needed to make things work, even if it wasn't always easy.

Ronnie wrote "Bring the House Down" and "Then Came the White Man" which scored him lots of points with the First Nations women we encountered across the country. Ronnie was a natural frontman. He lived to entertain. I probably spent more time with Ronnie than anyone in the band. He was never reluctant to take things to the edge, then take one more step just to see what would happen. He was like the kid who would convince the rest of us to leave the comfort of our block; that guy whose ability to cajole could always save the day if anything went wrong. By the end of a show, if there was a fan-favourite, it was probably Ronnie.

Though over-simplified, Richard, Kim and Ronnie gave The Stampeders smarts, heart, and soul. Perhaps this explains how three very different people made such a successful partnership.

PARTY TIME

In smaller communities, the local police, motel operators, and even restaurants weren't always welcoming to touring rock bands. However, the "lock up your daughters and get out the sniffer dogs" mentality was never extended to The Stampeders. It was more like, "the police chief's mom likes your music, so you guys are OK."

The idea of partying hard after a gig with girls pulled from the crowd was the exception, never the rule. After a show, The Stampeders usually invited the crew, the opening acts, and many locals back to their hotel rooms. But once there, the main objective was to have a laugh.

We'd have different activities like nightly board-hockey tournaments with a gram of brown Lebanese for the prize. Sometimes, Ronnie and Kim would break out a ventriloquist routine where the smaller Kim would sit on Ronnie's lap and play the insult-dummy.

On one tour, our opening act was a "mentalist" named Eric Levinson. He got the gig because his dad owned the Budget rent-a-car franchises in Montreal and Moncton, so we got comped on a couple of Dodges. To say that Eric was iffy on stage would be a compliment. Mentalism is the art of suggestive magic and whenever Eric was on stage, he'd mangle his set-ups. Watching Eric was like watching someone nervously trying to tell a joke and giving away the punchline. Eric's "reveal" would be delivered with flop-sweat and stammering. Audiences which were supposed to marvel at what they just seen were often left wondering, "What was the point of all that?"

However, after a couple of beers back at the motel, "The Amazing Mind of Eric Levinson" was actually kind of amazing. Hypnotism was part of Eric's skill set and it turned out Kim and Ronnie were both susceptible to post-hypnotic suggestion. One time, Ronnie was programmed to ask "Who farted?" anytime anyone said "Kim." Meanwhile, Kim couldn't stop himself from shouting "Shut up" anytime he heard the name "Ronnie." Kim even continued doing this through the rest of the tour; hypnotism was just the excuse he needed.

Maybe it's a "Western thing", but The Stampeders tours fostered a sense of one big, happy family. They made everyone around them feel comfortable even in uncomfortable situations.

During one show in Campbellton, New Brunswick, the stars had aligned for a fantastic after-show party. The owner of the motel upgraded three of our rooms to a two-storey guest house with a full kitchen, large living room, and a fireplace. On this particular stretch of the New Brunswick coastline, it was lobster season. And Campbellton had a nursing school filled with young women from all over the province.

Barry Archer, Donald K Donald's other tour manager, and I were both working on the tour. The band agreed we could juggled the weekly budget for dressing room supplies to pay for our party. We knew that Donald was coming to make his traditional "surprise visit to the front lines" so we wanted to make sure it would be a night to remember.

After the show, we all pitched in to help the crew with the load-out and hurried back to the house. Soon the party was rocking. The place was filled with guests, a roaring fire, fresh-cooked lobster, and a full bar. Ronnie was working overtime to keep everybody entertained.

Barry and I ducked into a small room by the entrance to tidy up the settlement sheets. That's when we heard a thumping from the back of the house. The sound of heavy footsteps grew louder as they approached, accompanied by someone bellowing "Hey-Hey-Hey!"

Barry muttered, "What the fuck…"

We peeked outside and saw Donald bounding down the hallway wearing nothing but a pair of socks and yelling like Fat Albert. Our opening act, Lorence Hud, walked in the front door with a girl he'd met that day. Donald Tarlton was not a small man in either reputation or girth, so it's understandable Lorence froze when he saw this large mass of determined flesh barrelling toward him.

"Get outta my way!" yelled Donald.

But it was too late. Lorence and his date were bowled over. Donald made a sharp right into the party room and scuttled around in his socks. He accidentally cornered himself but then deftly escaped by clambering over a couch. Barry and I stepped back so he could make his getaway, even though nobody was chasing him.

The nursing students quickly reached for their coats as Kim Berly leapt into full damage-control. "Don't worry... It's just Donald. He's our crazy promoter... No, not really crazy, he's harmless. Sorry about that. Don't worry, it won't happen again..."

Everyone settled back down and the party returned to normal. Lorence Hud still looked a bit incredulous, but he often looked that way. Barry and I returned to finish our paperwork, but no sooner had we sat down when we heard the thundering footsteps and a hearty "Hey-Hey-Hey!" again.

Donald apparently decided one good turn deserved another. But this time, he took off his socks for better traction. He followed the same path into the main room, pattered around the startled nursing students, got stuck in the corner again, and did some sort of sliding barrel-roll over the couch. And with a final "Hey-Hey-Hey!" he was gone.

The party was beyond salvation. By the time a fully-dressed Donald returned, just about everyone had left except for some pissed-off musicians and roadies.

"Where did everybody go?" Donald asked.

"You scared them all away," hissed Kim. "What were you thinking?"

It was a fair question. Maybe streaking was something Donald had always thought about doing, and what better place than this isolated corner of New Brunswick? Or maybe he was revealing his true intentions when he cheerfully said, "Oh well. I guess there's more lobster for us."

IAN THOMAS AND THE ORIGINS OF "THE GREAT WHITE NORTH"

Perhaps the best opening act on The Stampeders' tours was The Ian Thomas Band. Every player in the band was session-calibre. They had four terrific voices and could whip off a

Beach Boys medley which sounded as good as the Beach Boys. They also had Ian Thomas's songwriting which provided international hits for groups like Starship, Santana and Manfred Mann's Earth Band. But Ian also brought something else to the table: comedy.

During their set, we would all stop whatever we were doing so we could join the audience to hear Ian introduce the guys in his band. It was a hilarious five to ten-minute improvisation which was different at every performance. But I think his greatest comedic achievement took shape on a day where we made the twelve-hour jump from Thunder Bay to Sault Ste. Marie.

Ian Thomas, Ronnie King, and Kim Berly were travelling with me at the wheel. We decided to get about seventy-five miles behind us before stopping for breakfast at the Husky gas station near Nipigon. While waiting for the fried eggs, Ian was listening in on a conversation between two local teenagers. They sounded distinctively "hoser", which is a cadence often heard in small-town Canada.

They were looking out the window at a car that was gassing up. "Jeez, will you have a look at that red Charger, eh?" said the first one. "Whattaya think she's got under the hood?"

The other replied, "Don't torture yourself, eh? You couldn't touch a car like that with a ten-foot pole."

"Ah, take off, eh? Why do you have to be so mean anyways?"

"Cause you're a hoser, that's why."

The first teen reflects on this and, smiling, says, "Yeah, I guess so."

After breakfast and for the next few hours on our way to the Sault, we heard "Take off, eh?" and "Hoser!" about a hundred times from Ian. Ronnie and I kept egging him on but Kim, who had much less tolerance for stupidity, begged Ian to give it a rest. That might have been the end of it.

A couple of years later, Ian's older brother Dave Thomas and Rick Moranis were asked to create a recurring skit for their TV show, S.C.T.V. They needed a couple extra minutes for the Canadian version of the show because the American telecast was running more commercials.

"So, you want a skit that's just for Canada?" asked Rick. He turned to Dave, "Why don't we try something with those hoser guys your brother is always going on about?"

The result was one of the most definitively Canadian sketch-comedy segments ever created. *The Great White North* featured two brothers, Bob and Doug McKenzie, hosting a cable-access show in Canada. Bob and Doug would sit on a couch dressed in plaid shirts, hunting jackets, and toques, and talk about urgent subjects like long underwear and back bacon (or anything else that came to mind). The set was adorned with Molson Canadian beer cases, artificial plants, and a large map of North America with "GREAT WHITE NORTH" printed on the Canadian portion.

This show, which has undoubtedly inspired countless comedy segments including *Wayne's World* and even *Between Two Ferns*, was born at a gas station diner in Nipigon, Ontario when Ian Thomas "identified" the McKenzie Brothers as two young men you might encounter anywhere in rural Canada.

RECKLESS EDDY

At the other end of the spectrum the least competent opening act was me.

Before my first tour with The Stampeders, Donald pulled me into his office to have a chat. He explained that the tour would be playing small rooms with limited gross potentials. Our chances of working larger, more extensive tours with

The Stampeders in the future would depend on how profitable this "little" tour would be.

So he asked, "What's the cheapest opening act we can get?"

This was the kind of problem Donald loved to solve.

I suggested, "Ross Holloway would probably want thirty-five dollars a show and his own room." As a bonus for us, Ross was an artist on Aquarius who had a "turntable hit" called "Mostly New Days."

"No, that's too much," Donald objected.

If that was too much, I was out of suggestions and turned to leave.

"Wait a minute! You used to sing in Floyd Jones, right?"

I said, "I usually sang back-ups."

He didn't care. As far as he was concerned, I could play the guitar (I actually played the bass), I could sort of sing, and I was already going to be there. I absolutely did not want to do this. Between all the production, closing the advance sales outlets, the box office, the catering, the settlement with all the suppliers, *and* doing our books, there was no way I'd be able to perform. But Donald was persistent. He offered me a union card and $150 to buy a new guitar.

"And I'll pay you ten bucks a show," he said.

"Fifteen!" I countered.

"Done."

"Shit", I thought. I had a month to learn how to be an entertainer.

"Wait, I need to know your stage name."

"What's wrong with my name?" I asked.

"Well if it turns out you stink, I still need you to be my tour manager."

This made sense. I said, "Call me *Reckless Eddy.*"

I didn't know why I said that. I might have been inspired by Eddy Shack, a Toronto Maple Leaf who played the game with a reckless disregard for his well-being. I unconsciously named my act after a guy whose best move might have been crashing into the goalie.

On the tour, I quickly learnt that whenever the audience wasn't happy to see me, which was normal, I could make a deal with them. I would explain to the crowd that I had to perform for forty minutes. They would usually groan. But if they behaved, I would reward them by shortening my show. Some audiences would be so happy when I announced my closing number, "Another Man's Hair on My Razor", they would cheer loudly. Back in the headliner's dressing room it must have sounded like I was really warming up the crowd.

Reckless Eddy even got to release a single. This wasn't due to any effort on my part. It was just bad planning. Flush with the success of three consecutive Platinum albums, The Stampeders had a generous budget for their fourth L.P. which would be entitled *New Day*. There was an elaborate track by Richard Dodson entitled "Lorraine" which was as an homage to the swing era and featured a big-band arrangement. The horn section alone pushed the session and arrangement fees beyond anything the band had done before. Unfortunately, after the sessions were recorded, the band realized that nobody could sing the melody in that key.

This wasn't the first time either. Their signature hit "Sweet City Woman" was arranged in a key too high for anyone to sing. Changing the key would lose those great open strings in the guitar part. Richard solved the problem by re-tuning the guitars (and banjo), dropping everything by two semi-tones. On stage, he would always have a specially-tuned Telecaster just for "Sweet City Woman."

"Lorraine", with its expensive horn section was already "in the can" was not such an easy fix. But The Stampeders were not about to write off their investment.

After spending months trying to find a Toronto-based crooner who could record a new lead vocal, Kim suggested, "Reckless would have no trouble singing this an octave higher." Turns out, he was right.

I never attempted to perform my single onstage. As Reckless Eddy, I never had the luxury of performing with a skillful guitar player, never mind a full horn section. But thanks to pure serendipity, "Release a single," was one item I could check off my bucket list.

JIMMY LEROY

I think I speak for the entire Stampeders family when I say the most lovable opening act was Jimmy Leroy. James Leroy and Denim had one big hit, "A Touch of Magic." But the group had other tracks which got lots of radio airplay in Canada. Jimmy had a big voice and the band was comprised of some of the top players in Ottawa. But what audiences likely remembered most about James Leroy and Denim, was Jimmy's sense of theatrics. One night on his first tour with The Stampeders, we decide to have a little fun at his expense.

The setting was the Arts and Culture Centre in Cornerbrook, Newfoundland, which featured a donation from the government of Czechoslovakia. It was the "Lanterna Magica" rig from the Czech pavilion at Expo '67. The rig had a ceiling-to-floor stage-wide screen, made of some remarkable weave which radiated a rainbow of colours when light passed over it. It also had a set of lights and backing screen which turned it into the perfect medium for performing in silhouette. We discovered this wonder at soundcheck and hatched a plan for the show that evening.

Jimmy had a song called "Friends and Brothers" which he would always introduce with a story. The story was about

Jimmy's relationship with his brother and all the good times they had before he died. Each performance, the story grew longer. In real life, Jimmy didn't have a brother but he was so good at storytelling, people in the audience would be tearing-up before he launched into the song.

In Cornerbrook, Jimmy told his emotional story with the Lanterna Magica aglow at the back of the stage. When he started the song, the audience saw the outline of what might be Frankenstein, slowly carrying a dead body in his arms across the screen. It was Ronnie carrying Kim. The two of them were able to double-back behind a scrim so by the time Jimmy got to the first chorus, the two Stampeders could make the same passage, this time with Kim draped over Ronnie's shoulder.

For the next pass, Ronnie carried Kim the same way, but Frankenstein was now swaying in time with the music. For the fourth pass, we had attached roped to a small wheeled platform so that we could make it look as if Ronnie, still carrying Kim, was floating across the stage. On the final pass, the crew pulled on the ropes hard so that Ronnie and Kim flew across the screen while Kim waved to the audience.

Jimmy knew his performance was getting a strange reaction. Since it was his first show on "The Rock", maybe he initially attributed it to a language barrier. He had never evoked laughter with this song. By Ronnie and Kim's fourth pass behind the screen, even his band was cracking up. Jimmy saw the final pass just as the audience burst into applause (well before the end of the song).

After the set, Jimmy couldn't seem to decide if he was wounded or furious. In the end, he conceded it might be an idea to do it every night. But the Lanterna Magica equipment was only in Cornerbrook.

The following year, James and Denim were with us on a string of dates out West. At the beginning of their leg, Jimmy called us together for an announcement. He had been diagnosed with diabetes. He lugubriously explained how this meant "a sad goodbye" to his two great passions; pizza and scotch. Then he immediately back-pedaled, suggesting "abstinence" might be over-doing things. However, he made me promise I would fine him twenty-five dollars if he ate any pizza.

Of course, within the first week, the Stampeders' crew spotted a pizza delivery guy heading to the second floor of the hotel in Nelson, B.C. On a hunch, they trailed him straight to Jimmy's room. In the time it took to organize our intervention, Jimmy had polished off half the pie. True to his word, though, he gave us twenty-five bucks and the rest of the pizza.

I believe those tours with the Stampeders were some of James Leroy's happiest times. Nobody enjoyed being a kid in a playground more than James Leroy. It turned out he would part company with Denim not long after the end of the tour. He would never have another hit single. How much these heady times differed from his lonelier hours came into terrible focus when I got the news in 1979. Jimmy had committed suicide in an Ottawa hotel room. He was thirty-two.

WALTER

One of The Stampeders' more difficult opening acts was Walter Rossi. He recorded three albums for Aquarius Records and the second, *Six Strings Nine Lives*, deservedly won two Juno Awards (the Canadian equivalent of a Grammy). However, most people have never heard the album, which is a real shame because everything about it was remarkable.

Walter was a quiet man who was fiercely proud of his
art. His approach to making music was so passionate, he was
insulted if people were merely indifferent. He had a faint
Italian accent when he sang, and a problem with stuttering
when he spoke. Walter thought the Stampeders were care-
less and lazy, two things he certainly wasn't, and he believed
opening for Stampeders' audiences was "casting pearls
before swine."

One night in Newcastle, New Brunswick, Walter ignored
me when I told him to wrap up his soundcheck. We had a big
crowd outside, and it was raining. After telling him a second
time, I went to the other end of the building and opened
the doors.

To speed things along, I helped tear tickets. Suddenly, I was
tackled from behind. I rolled over and saw Walter on top of
me. Walter looked like he could have been cast as a biker in
a Quinn Martin cop show, complete with his bearded scowl
and a black leather jacket. Meanwhile, a real cop had rushed
over and was raising his flashlight. I yelled, "Don't hurt him!"
just before it came crashing down. The cop escorted Walter
back to his dressing room.

Walter's anger continued to simmer as the tour went along.
He started killing a mickey of Southern Comfort before
every show. When we played at Sault Memorial Gardens
toward the end of Walter's segment of the tour, he decided to
tell a joke on stage about how he felt being the opening act.
Between the Southern Comfort and his stuttering, nobody
got the joke.

"So you didn't like my joke," he said. "What do you think
about this?"

He proceeded to glare at the crowd in silence. After *several
minutes*, booing began. I was headed for the house lights, but
his band launched into a song.

Earlier, I had asked Luffy, who was mixing the sound for Walter's sets, to tape the show. I meant to give it to Walter as a happy surprise, but after his "joke", I had a change of plans. The next night we were in North Bay. North Bay was a communications centre for N.O.R.A.D. and a couple of times every minute, our P.A. system would react to the military radio signals and emit a loud "Beep." It was something like the gig at the air force base in the movie *Spinal Tap*. This always happened in North Bay. We expected it.

I told Walter to wait in his dressing room while we tried to fix this "bug." We obviously couldn't, but Walter didn't know. However, this seemed like the perfect opportunity for Walter to reflect on his behaviour. I asked Luffy to play the recording of last night's show through the sound system. It hadn't even gotten to "the joke" before Walter came running out of the dressing room, raging at me to turn off the tape. I gave him the cassette and told him he could start his soundcheck.

That night, Walter didn't drink before his set. The following night, Walter played his last show on the tour in Sudbury. It was amazing.

BREAKING THE DEADLOCK

Working with The Stampeders was a lot of fun. The band pioneered a grassroots, distinctively Canadian version of Arena Rock. But ultimately, the party ended.

I have no doubt there was a fatigue factor; each year the grind of touring gets a little harder, especially when the prospect of success seems to be slipping away. But in my view, the ultimate undoing of The Stampeders had to do with the sharing of wealth.

If their overall finances are viewed as pie and with each person getting a piece, the pie seemed to be getting smaller every year. What's more, not everybody was getting the same amount of pie.

There were only so many sources of income for a rock musician. Record royalties are easy to overestimate, especially when the market is as small as Canada. Also, recording artists signed to labels had to repay all recording costs and advances at *their* royalty rate before they see any actual royalties. The labels might rake in the dough, but an artist could have a Platinum Album in Canada (100,000 sales in those days) and still not earn record royalties.

The Stampeders and their manager Mel Shaw were in better shape than most artists because they owned their own label. They had to pay recording costs, pressing costs, marketing costs, songwriting royalties and a distribution fee out of the sales revenues. But the rest was theirs. Even then, The Stampeders might clear just over a dollar an album.

However, the recordings made The Stampeders popular enough to tour. The shows I managed might gross as much as a million dollars in one "short" sixty-stop tour. But after expenses, the band might only net a third of that. My guess is being a Stampeder earned each guy about five times my salary. But this was probably a far cry from what fans thought famous rock musicians were earning.

If you were also a successful songwriter, you had a second income. "Mechanical Royalties" are paid to the songwriters on every copy sold. Mind you, in those days that amount was only two cents a song (which was usually shared with a publisher). There was also "synch money", which came from placing songs in movies, TV shows, and commercials, though this kind of income wasn't as common or substantial as it is today. Finally, there were "Performance Royalties", mostly paid by radio stations. These could be very substantial.

Ronnie once lamented to me that when the songwriting cheques arrived every six months, Richard, who wrote all the big hits, could go out and buy a new car. Kim, who had written a couple of mid-sized hits, could make the down payment on a new car. Meanwhile, Ronnie, who wrote a few album tracks, could go out with his girlfriend and buy a steak dinner.

Mel Shaw, the band's manager, knew Richard's songs were the key to the band's success. Whenever the band had to make a decision, Mel would side with Richard and there would be a deadlock. In what I saw as a plan to marginalize Richard, Ronnie managed to increase the size of the band with members who would support his point of view.

On the next Stampeders album *Platinum*, they added a second drummer, a second guitarist, two horns and a keyboardist. For touring, this meant the size of the road crew would also need to double. The old, smaller operation could make money in most rooms with five hundred paying customers. With at least a dozen people on the road, the ticket prices and crowd sizes had to increase.

However, for that to happen, the band needed continued radio success. Richard had come up with a couple of pop gems, "Baby with You" and "Looking Back". But Ronnie was leading the charge to make The Stampeders "funkier." The new band members, though they were only sidemen, also had a say in the song selection, so Richard's compositions were rejected as being too "saccharine." That was when Richard Dodson quit.

Without Richard, the lead-off single on *Platinum* was an extended vamp written by Ronnie called "Bring the House Down." The continuous repetitive musical figure, usually without much in the way of a chord progression, was a far cry from the well-loved Stampeders music. Imagine an up-tempo

James Brown song performed by The Stampeders. It could make for an interesting live performance, but the track made no sense to Canadian radio in 1977.

The six previous Stampeders studio albums had all cracked the national Top 25. The optimistically titled *Platinum* didn't make the Top 100.

On tour, the most popular songs at Stampeders' concerts were still the Rich Dodson compositions. For The Stampeders to deliberately lose Richard was like Wings thinking they'd do better without Paul McCartney. Richard never exuded coolness nor embraced the idea of being a rock star. However, it took two guitarists to replace him and the band never wrote another great song. It's even hard to picture The Stampeders without the dude in the cowboy hat and that red double-neck Gibson guitar.

The three original Stampeders re-united in the early '90s with Richard and his wife, Mary-Lynn, running the show. Since then, they play 20 to 40 shows most years. They are "soft-ticket" shows, that is, annual fairs or festivals with built-in audiences; a far cry from the 400+ shows I did with the band.

Playing every conceivable market from coast-to-coast, year after year back in the '70s wasn't only a sign of the band's success; it contributed to the band's enduring popularity. We were just trying to make a buck. But if we set out to make The Stampeders something meaningful to a generation of Canadians, we couldn't have had a better plan.

CHAPTER SIX

APRIL WINE

DISCLAIMER: I MET APRIL WINE almost as soon as they arrived in Montreal. I was working in a bar where they hoped to find work. Within a couple of years I was touring with them and promoting their records. Ultimately I would even become the head of their label (although that was after the group disbanded). My impressions of the other artists discussed in this book are just that: impressions. In the case of April Wine, their story and mine are intertwined. I got to observe and sometimes share in their many ups and downs. This is why you might find this chapter is different from the others.

AQUARIUS RECORDS

By the late 1960's Toronto's 1050-CHUM was Canada's most important Top 40 radio station. CHUM's management was considering how to deal with the impending Canadian Content Regulations. Rules requiring Canada's radio to play more Canadian music seemed inevitable. The stations closer to the American border were worried that being forced to play this "CanCon" would put them at a disadvantage. But the folks at CHUM were considering how they might benefit.

They decided it was time to get into the record business. In 1969 they launched MUCH Productions and partnered with a music publisher named Brian Chater. Brian went looking for the talent and came up with two Montreal artists: Michel Pagliaro and April Wine.

Stan Klees, who was the co-owner of Canada's music trade magazine RPM, raised a concern. Stan pointed out that if CHUM ever played an artist signed to MUCH Productions, this would be a clear conflict of interest. Yes, CHUM might favour its own artists, but what if the government agreed with Stan and CHUM was not allowed to play its own recordings? The real victims would be Michel Pagliaro and April Wine. They could never get played on the most popular radio station in the country.

CHUM decided to hedge its bet and roll the dice with Pagliaro. His album, released on the MUCH label, produced three hits singles, "Lovin' You Ain't Easy", "Rainshowers" and "Some Sing Some Dance". But Brian Chater and Terry Flood worked out a deal where April Wine's albums would be licensed to Aquarius Records.

Aquarius was a new label started by Terry, Donald and Bob. Like the folks at MUCH, they saw CanCon as a game-changer for Canadian artists. Since they had no experience in the record business, they joined forces with Jack and Dan Lazare. The Lazare brothers' Les Disques Gamma was the hottest indie label in Montreal. Its roster included two of Quebec's biggest stars, Gilles Vigneault and Robert Charlebois.

Aquarius was not an instant success. But it would go on to sell many millions of records. Until Corey Hart came along, thirteen years later, most Aquarius sales (and virtual all of its profits) were generated by April Wine. It's certain that without April Wine there would be no Aquarius Records. It's also possible that without Aquarius Records there would be no April Wine. And if not for CanCon, I'm not so sure how any of this could have played out.

HOUSE-CLEANING

In 1971, not long after Laugh-In closed its doors, April Wine's self-titled debut album was released. One song, "Fast Train", got played on the radio in most parts of Canada. But the next album, *On Record*, had three national hits.

The first was a cover of a song by England's Hot Chocolate, "You Could Have Been a Lady." Then came an Elton John B-side, "Bad Side of the Moon." These two songs opened doors at radio stations for "Drop Your Guns", which was written by David Henman. With three radio hits in a row, April Wine could make a triumphant return home to the Maritimes in 1972 as a headline act.

While on that tour, I learned about the tension between a founding member, drummer Ritchie Henman, and the new bassist, Jimmy Clench. (Recall that the original bass player, Jimmy Henman left the band in 1971.)

The rhythm section is supposed to be a tightly synchronized unit – the drummer provides the rhythm and percussion, and the bass player drives the beat. Jimmy Clench was doing a fine job. His playing was full of ideas but never at the expense of the song's pulse. By contrast, Ritchie's rhythm occasionally tended to accelerate. He seemed unaware of this and would say things like, "Jim, you came in a little late…" However, Jimmy felt the problem was Ritchie's inability to "sit in the pocket"; that is, maintain a steady tempo.

This tension came to a head at a show in Stratford, Ontario. After once again being blamed for "coming in late", Jimmy smashed a beer bottle on the floor. He yelled, "I'm gonna kill the fucker!" and lunged at Ritchie. Luckily, Myles and David jumped in before anything could happen.

That same year, a band called Elf opened a show in Sudbury. The leader of the group, Ronnie James Dio, visited the April Wine's dressing room later that evening and told them, "You guys are a good rock band. Once you replace your drummer, you should do well in America." The minute he left the room, Jimmy exploded. "I'm telling you! We need a new drummer!" However, Jimmy wouldn't get his wish just yet.

In the winter of 1972-73, the band went to work preparing for their third studio album *Electric Jewels*. Myles Goodwyn and Jimmy Clench announced they were a songwriting team. Meanwhile, producer Ralph Murphy, who came up with both "You Could Have Been a Lady" and "Bad Side of the Moon" for April Wine's previous album, found a song called "Weeping Widow" for the new album. David Henman, who wrote April Wine's only original hit to date, was excited about a new song he had written called "Walkin' to Frisco." But the recording sessions were put on hold, in part because the new Goodwyn-Clench team wanted more time to work on the material. Instead of making a record, the band went on another Maritime tour.

The decision to delay the recording may have been strategic. By this time, Myles had emerged as the leader of April Wine. Any decision about how to handle the rift between Jimmy Clench and Ritchie Henman rested with Myles. If the decision was to change drummers, it might be best to make the move before completing a new album.

April Wine had purchased a second-hand Cadillac limousine which they would take on their Maritime tour. Being a car fanatic, Ritchie claimed his spot behind the wheel. He even bought a chauffeur's cap and jacket. Myles believed that when the band traveled together, it should only be the band.

However, with a glass partition separating the front and back compartments, Ritchie felt the front seat was his own private domain; a place to enjoy a cheroot and the company of his girlfriend. He was literally distancing himself from the rest of the band by driving the car. Meanwhile, Myles and new songwriting partner Jimmy Clench were in the back planning the future.

At the end of this Maritime tour, Ritchie was replaced by Jerry Mercer. David Henman was asked to stay on, but left out of loyalty to his brother. He was replaced by Gary Moffet who had been in a band called Pops Merrily. Although April Wine would always be identified with Halifax, three of the four members of the band were now from Montreal.

The "Electric Jewels" album was completed. Its title-track represented the zeitgeist of April Wine in 1973, or at least Myles' headspace at the time. It was a musical rant against the band's label and management. The band, (the "electric jewels") *was controlled by fools*. And since "fools" was plural, it seemed Myles was upset with a list of people. However, the only one who seemed to take the message personally was Terry Flood.

Terry was the president and co-owner of Aquarius, but first and foremost he was April Wine's manager. So when Myles hired a lawyer to negotiate a new contract with the label, Terry made sure Myles got the recording and publishing deals he wanted.

Meanwhile Ritchie and David Henman formed a band called Silver before going their separate ways. David launched David and the Debutantes and Ritchie joined The Wackers. A year later, the Henman brothers were reunited and, along with Bob Segarini, Kootch Trochim, Wayne Cullen and future April Wine guitarist Brian Greenway, formed a band called The Dudes.

CAPTAIN BRING-DOWN AND HIS ELECTRIC ADVENTURE

The only year between 1972 and 1980 when April Wine didn't release a new studio album was 1974. That was the year April Wine did its first coast-to-coast concert tour. It was also the year when Lloyd Brault firmly established himself as April Wine's "captain."

With their first national tour in the planning stages, road manager Lloyd Brault and his younger brother Kenny designed a stage lighting concept called The Electric Adventure. When April Wine added Jerry Mercer to the band, they acquired "Beamer's" famous drum solo from the Mashmakhan show. Years down the road when I was president of Aquarius records, I met Garth Brooks and found out he had always loved April Wine. He claimed, "I would hitch-hike across two states to see those guys." He said his live show owed more to April Wine and Kiss than any Country band. Then he asked, "Is that drummer with the bald head and laser light still around?"

Besides the drum solo, another staple of April Wine's show was a mylar-covered cannon. Towards the end of their set, this functioning replica of a naval cannon covered in shiny mylar blasted *flaming confetti* into the audience. You'd think the people down in front would object, but the opposite was true. Jimmy Clench would have to brace the cannon with his foot so it didn't recoil into the amp-line. However, if a roadie overdid the charge, which happened, a "loose cannon" could knock Jimmy on his ass. It was an exhilarating highlight of April Wine shows for years to come.

Lloyd and Kenny put a lot of thought into all of the visual effects. Each had a dramatic purpose and no effect was over-used. One loud explosion had far more impact than five or six, provided it was timed at the most unexpected (and preferably quiet) moment in the set. From the very start, the "Electric Adventure" would guarantee a crowd reaction.

Lloyd Brault also set an organizational standard which enabled April Wine to effortlessly upscale the operation over the years. He left a good job at Canadair to work with April Wine back in the Laugh-In days and would have a remarkable career in the music business, leaving April Wine at one point to work with The Guess Who. Wine would hire him back on better terms and he remained their guy until the band broke up in the mid-'80s. Lloyd would then go on to tour-manage acts like Pink Floyd, U-2, and Celine Dion.

One technique Lloyd used on the job was to deliberately "play dumb." If he ever seemed baffled, it generally meant he thought the other person was full of shit. This also made Lloyd particularly effective at a show settlements where he'd refuse to budge if he thought he was right (and he was seldom wrong). An hour after the trucks had driven away and the guy on the other side of the table was losing his shit to get out of the place, Lloyd would calmly light another cigarette and say "Let's go over this again." He could certainly be diplomatic but was also known for his bluntness. He never shied away from the truth, even when it would not go down well. That's why in the early '70s, Jimmy Clench once referred to Lloyd as "Captain Bring-down." After that, he became known in the Wine camp as "The Captain." In fact, Lloyd is "The Captain" referenced in the lyrics of the song, "Electric Jewels."

To prepare Canada for the Electric Adventure tour, the band recorded a live album to introduce the new line-up. It was recorded at the Queen Elizabeth High School Auditorium in Halifax and produced by two members of The Rascals, Dino Danelli and Gene Cornish. The recording engineer was Eddie Kramer. It would sell about 30,000 copies, which was great considering it only took a couple hours to record. And it was the first April Wine album to feature Jerry's famous drum solo. Along with *Electric Jewels*, *April Wine Live* enabled the band to become the second group, after the Stampeders, to headline one of D.K.D.'s coast-to-coast rock tours.

April Wine also received an unanticipated promotional boost just in time for the Electric Adventure Tour. As a "last stab" at the U.S. market, the band's American label came up with a song called "I'm on Fire for You Baby." The recording was personally produced by the owner of Big Tree Records, Doug Morris. Doug would go on to have an unbelievable career as the co-CEO at Atlantic Records and CEO of MCA Music, Universal Music, and Sony Music. Along the way, he also brought rap music to suburban shopping malls. Doug did a masterful job producing "I'm on Fire for You Baby" and Gary Moffet delivered his first of many stunning guitar solos. Unfortunately, the track failed to chart for Big Tree in America, but it was a very timely hit in Canada.

Prior to heading out on tour, April Wine was nominated for a Juno Award in what was then called the Best New Group category. By this time, the band had sold about 200,000 albums and scored five Top-Twenty hit singles (including a couple of Top-Tens). They were one of very few Canadian-based groups which could even contemplate headlining hockey arenas from coast to coast. Although the Juno went to a Toronto duo called Myles and Lenny, I feel like The Electric Adventure Tour established April Wine as Canada's best new group that year.

TWO STEPS FORWARD

In late 1974, April Wine went to work on their next album at the original Studio Tempo on McGill College Avenue in the heart of downtown Montreal. I sat in on most of the sessions and got to witness the recording their breakthrough album: *Stand Back*.

The credit on the album reads, "Produced by April Wine" but in reality, two songs were produced by Myles and Jimmy Clench, while all other songs were produced by Myles (though every track owed a great deal to engineer Ian Terry and his assistant Billy Szawlowski).

On their previous album *Electric Jewels,* the only original song which got a lot of radio play was "Lady Run, Lady Hide." Though credit was given to the Goodwyn-Clench partnership, the song was definitely more Goodwyn than Clench. However, because of their agreement, they got equal credit. It's possible this led Myles to rethink their partnership.

Jimmy had a couple of songs he'd written by himself for *Stand Back*. Myles said he needed more time for what he was working on, so they should start recording what Jimmy had already written. Once those songs were recorded, Myles and Jimmy would sit down together and finish the material Myles had developed.

"Oowatanite" was the first of Jimmy's songs they recorded. For the intro, Jerry Mercer took the bell from the studio's fire alarm system and mounted it on a cymbal stand. When the track was recorded, everyone knew this would be a great addition to the live set. But I'm not sure we realized it would become one of April Wine's trademark songs.

The band then worked on Jimmy's "Baby Done Got Some Soul." As the final overdub was completed, Myles revealed a surprise. He had already completed the other eight songs he intended for *Stand Back* and he was unilaterally dissolving the Goodwyn-Clench songwriting team.

Jimmy was furious. For a while he refused to come back to the studio. When he did return, it was clear this wouldn't be "water under the bridge" any time soon.

One consequence of Jimmy's walk-out was that I sang some back-up vocals, including "Don't Push Me Around", which was inspired by Kenny Brault. Myles originally intended for Jim to sing the high harmonies. This was another case where the top of my range was a little higher than anyone else in the room. Jimmy would later tell me he couldn't hit those high notes anyway, so I may have been called upon to sing the parts even if he had been there.

There were two Canadian hits, "Tonight is a Wonderful Time" and "I Wouldn't Want to Lose Your Love" but the quality of the entire album is the reason it sold over 200,000 copies in Canada and landed April Wine a deal with London Records in the United States.

Once winter ended and the tour season rolled around, I would only work certain segments of April Wine's 1975 national tour because I had a scheduling conflict with Stampeders dates. On the April Wine dates I did work, it was clear Jimmy had still not gotten over the way Myles had ended their songwriting partnership. Working together on the road seemed to fuel Jimmy's anger.

After a couple of beers at a gig, Jimmy would go on to have a couple more at the hotel. The Jimmy of old would have been feeling pretty mellow by this point. But just the opposite was happening. By two in the morning, Clench would be reverting to his catch-phrase, "I'm gonna kill the fucker." Except instead of talking about Ritchie Henman, he was now talking about Myles. His threats to Ritchie always seemed like bluster. In reality apart from their differences over tempo, they got along well. But when it came to Myles, Jimmy's anger was visceral and the threats more menacing.

When the tour ended, April Wine looked for a new bass player.

ONE STEP BACK

In the seventies it seemed like, every *second* April Wine album was successful. The "in-between" albums would often set them back. It was their second album *On Record* which put them on the map and then their fourth, *Stand Back* which took things to the next level. By the end of 1975, *Stand Back* was an undeniable success and the most recent tour had been the best yet. The future looked bright heading into 1976.

Myles chose Steve Lang to replace Jimmy Clench on bass. Steve had been in a Montreal band called Devotion. He had a busier style of playing than Clench. A good example of this can be found on April Wine's 1978 recording, "Hot on the Wheels of Love" which Steve co-wrote. But Steve Lang wasn't a strong singer which meant Myles was now the only lead vocalist.

Stand Back's success led to high expectations for the next album. Radio eagerly awaited the first single from *The Whole World's Goin' Crazy*. It turned out to be the title track which used a technique which had succeeded on the previous album. A track called "Slow Poke" used tape speed to lower Myles' voice, making him sound like a robotic Barry White. The result was a fun track which one New York disc jockey declared "the dirtiest song of all time." However, for this new single, they used tape speed to make Myle's voice higher. These vocals ended up sounding like Alvin and the Chipmunks had gotten into a stash of amphetamines. Though the single was an instant add at radio across Canada and the fastest April Wine single to ever enter the Top 10, listener feedback was tepid. In a matter of weeks, it dropped off the charts.

Because record retailers tended to order pallets of any follow-up to a big success, April Wine shipped over 200,000 copies of the new album. Though the album had good songs for the live show like "Gimme Love" and "So Bad", it didn't have a hit single. Retailers started counting down the mandatory sixty days until they could return the overstock. *The Whole World's Goin' Crazy* may have *shipped* double-platinum, but half the albums never sold.

Expectations were also high for an upgraded live show. The *Stand Back* album cover was inspired by the silver cannon created for The Electric Adventure tour. This time, the newest stage prop was inspired by the album cover. *The Whole World's Goin' Crazy* featured an illustration based on Mad Hatter from *Alice in Wonderland*. The tour featured a fifteen-foot-tall mechanized papier-mâché Mad Hatter.

"Hedley," as he was called, was so big he had to be transported horizontally in his own truck and so fragile he needed delicate handling. Once Hedley got going on-stage, he would move one arm while emitting light and fog. But Hedley was no explosive Mylar-covered cannon. Even when he functioned properly, the effect was more like a parade float than anything which would get a roar from a rock crowd.

Although the album was a disappointment, the tour did good business. April Wine's live show was strong enough to survive a shaky album. Unfortunately, the American release by London Records went nowhere. The plan had been to support radio success in the United States with lots of tour dates. However, the lack of airplay meant there would be no American tour. It was beginning to look like April Wine might be one of those Canadian bands which were big in Canada but would never enjoy real success in the United States.

GOODIE TWO-SHOES

Following the 1976 tour, Myles decided to take some time away from April Wine and record a solo album. The title track was a big band jazz instrumental entitled "Goodie Two-Shoes." The variety of styles on his record was a complete departure from April Wine. Besides the jazzy title track, there were a couple of Caribbean-inspired songs, some Country-flavoured material and even a novelty song where Myles wrote new lyrics to the old Jimmy Dean song, "Big Bad John." There was the beautiful "Child's Garden", the very personal "Marjorie" which was about the mother Myles lost as a child, and one of his earliest attempts at songwriting, "You Won't Dance with Me".

Everything about *Goodie Two Shoes,* including the album art, was approved and set to go. But before pulling the trigger, Terry called a meeting with the band to lay out a sobering thought. If April Wine didn't have a new album, they would be touring in 1977 without anything new on the radio or in the stores. And no one needed to be reminded how the last album had under-performed. There was a risk everything they had worked for during the past five years might waft away.

Terry proposed repurposing Myles' solo album to be an April Wine release. Myles must have been concerned. He worked hard to make an album which didn't sound like April Wine, and he succeeded. Would fans even accept it as an *April Wine* album? The only familiar element was Myles' voice. Terry asked if Myles had any new "April Wine-type songs" the band could record. "Forever for Now" was a song Myles had in mind for some future April Wine session. It would have to do. It was quickly recorded and replaced the jazzy "Goodie Two Shoes" to become the title track of the next April Wine album.

The *Forever for Now* album must have come as quite a surprise to April Wine fans. But a surprise to the rest of us was "You Won't Dance with Me", a song Myles had written about ten years earlier, would become April Wine's best-selling single, ever. It even carried the album to Gold status.

There was some doubt if *Forever for Now* would be strong enough to support April Wine's tour plans, but there would be a couple of unexpected developments before the band toured in 1977.

The Rolling Stones were planning on recording a live album at Toronto's El Mocambo Tavern. They wanted the room packed with fans but they also wanted their appearance to be a surprise. Since the 1972 Rolling Stones bombing at the Montreal Forum, Stones' manager Peter Rudge had developed a friendship with Donald. The two cooked up a free ticket giveaway with CHUM-FM which could easily fill the room for two consecutive nights in March. The billing promised April Wine with special guest, The Cockroaches. But when audiences arrived, they were treated to April Wine opening for the Rolling Stones.

Eddie Kramer (who recorded the April Wine's *Live* album in 1974) was engineering the Stones' live sessions, so it was arranged for him to also record April Wine at the El Mocambo. They would record some of the April Wine standards like "Oowatanite", "Don't Push Me Around" and "You Could Have Been a Lady", but also a couple never-released Wackers songs contributed by Bob Segarini; "Teenage Love" and "Juvenile Delinquent."

Live at the El Mocambo fell short of the "Gold" standard, but it enhanced the band's profile. On their summer tour, their stage was decorated with fake palm trees to evoke the "El Mo" cover art.

The other development for that tour was the addition of a third guitarist. Nicknamed "The Kid", Brian Greenway had been in M.I.C. when Jimmy Golightly was their manager. He was also in the version of Mashmakhan that appeared at the

Maple Music Junket's Massey Hall show and played along-side the Henman Brothers in The Dudes. Brian became the second lead vocalist and wrote a couple of songs which April Wine recorded. He also played the harmonica. As a guitarist, Brian brought fluid, blues-infused soloing style to the band. This new three lead guitar format was not unique, but it was distinctive and gave April Wine fresh energy.

Myles Goodwyn, Jerry Mercer, Garry Moffet, Steve Lang, and Brian Greenway became the April Wine lineup which would become world-famous. This 1977 tour was also the last time I toured with April Wine as a D.K.D. tour manager.

FLASH-FORWARD

Flash-forward to the year 2010. April Wine is being announced as the newest inductees into the Canadian Music Hall of Fame during Juno Weekend in St. John's Newfoundland. Myles Goodwyn takes the stage with Brian Greenway and reads a statement. He names and thanks many past members including the three Henmans who formed the band, but were gone by 1973. Myles also gives thanks to several others who played in different versions of the April Wine which re-formed in the '90s. At these Hall of Fame functions, it's not unusual for a band member to be absent. But in this case, it was most of the April Wine that people remember.

By 2010, Jim Clench wasn't doing so well. He was entering the last seven months of a losing battle with lung cancer. But Jim was born in Newfoundland and would later be buried there, so it's likely he would have made an effort to be in his home province that Juno Weekend if he'd been asked. But even setting Jimmy Clench aside, where were Jerry Mercer, Gary Moffet, and Steve Lang? What's the story?

Let's consider why the band was inducted in the first place.
By far, the main reason for April Wine's success is Myles
Goodwyn. His leadership and talent are beyond question.
Brian Greenway elevated the band the moment he walked
on their stage and added a third dimension to April Wine's
guitar arsenal. But Myles never made Brian a full-fledged
member of the band. He was always a "hired gun" whereas
Jerry, Gary and Steve were partners in the group. I also think
many would agree April Wine may not be Hall of Famers
if you stopped the clock in 1977. It was the three albums
April Wine made between 1978 and 1981 which punched
that ticket, and the making of those albums was very much a
group effort.

In 1978, *First Glance* was the first April Wine album
released internationally by Capitol Records. It got off to a
poor start when the all-important first single, "Rock n' Roll
is a Vicious Game", failed to chart in America. The follow-up,
"Comin' Right Down on Top of Me", didn't even do that
well in Canada. But nine months after the release of *First
Glance,* Aquarius released a third single. That song, "Roller",
became a hit in Canada and shot across the Strait of Detroit
and blew up in the United States. *First Glance* turned out to
be a success after all.

The 1979 album, *Harder... Faster*, did even better on the
strength of the anthem, "I Like to Rock". In that same year,
April Wine's Greatest Hits was released in Canada. It would
eventually sell 400,000 copies. The following studio album,
The Nature of the Beast, would be the group's best-selling
album of all time and would establish April Wine as headlin-
ers outside of Canada. The albums April Wine released during
this four-year period would sell roughly five million copies.

However, the 1983 album *Powerplay* failed to impress.
Perhaps this was predictable, and maybe even overdue. The

band tended to release successes with every *second* album. *Powerplay* ended the band's longest streak of hit albums. Two songs, "Anything You Want, You Got It" and "Enough is Enough", were popular in Canada, but in the United States, they only got airplay if the station was promoting an upcoming April Wine tour date. This latest album was a setback which would prove to be a turning point.

Myles and British producer Mike Stone worked together on *Nature of the Beast* and *Powerplay* and reunited for the next album, *Animal Grace*. Meanwhile, a rift between Myles and the rest of the band was developing. This was exacerbated when Myles decided he needed a two-week *timeout* mid-session. With the studio sitting empty, and the clock ticking at rate of $500 per day, the other members of April Wine decided to use the downtime to record some ideas they had for new songs.

When Myles returned to Le Studio, he saw the band's demos as an affront to his creative authority. Myles started curtailing their involvement to the point they were only welcome at the studio if they were actually needed to record a part. Myles would later suggest the other guys in the band didn't appreciate the weight he carried as the songwriter, arranger, and producer. However, he also admitted to a substance abuse problem around this time.

Myles and Mike Stone eventually completed *Animal Grace,* but it was an ordeal. They used up all their time at Le Studio Morin Heights and ended up moving to the even more expensive Electric Ladyland Studio in New York. The album's budget was US$350,000 (about a million bucks in today's money), and they still went over budget.

It's said the hardest part of producing a record is the hundreds of decisions that have to be made quickly. Judging from the cartons of tapes that came back from New York, Myles and Mike were struggling to make any. There were numerous mixes of every track. There were over twenty versions of "Sons of the Pioneers." It would take several hours just to listen to all the mixes of that one song.

Worst of all, the sound of the final mastered release was overly processed. The playing was uninspired to the point of being mechanical. Myles' vocals sounded like he was ailing from chronic nasal congestion.

Animal Grace marked the first time an April Wine album was shunned by Canadian radio.

Because of the album's colossal failure, the only income the band members could expect would come from playing live. After the next tour was announced and tickets were already on sale, Myles issued an ultimatum. Not only would this be their *final tour*, but he would only go on stage if the others signed over all rights they had as members of April Wine. The band had to choose between cancelling the tour or going ahead and hoping something could be worked out.

About five shows into the Animal Grace Tour, Myles produced the paperwork. His deal allowed the band to continue earning record royalties from past recordings. But because *Animal Grace* didn't sell enough to cover a small fraction of its cost, the royalties from all April Wine albums would go towards repaying the debt for years to come. And if Myles' deal wasn't signed by the time the gates opened that night at the Kingswood Amphitheatre, he was heading home.

When the tour finally limped into Vancouver, Myles announced to the mere 1200 fans at the P.N.E. Coliseum this would be the last time April Wine would be coming to town. He said the band would be happy to shake hands with everybody as soon as the show was over. That's pretty much what happened. Once the house lights came up, the group went down into the pit and hundreds of B.C. fans lined up to say goodbye. That's the last time I saw the group together. The final tour date was a couple of days later on July 31st in Kelowna. But April Wine was effectively dissolved, at the insistence of Myles Goodwyn, on July 16th, 1984 in Toronto. After the tour, Jerry, Gary, and Steve were out of April Wine.

Myles would make one last "April Wine" album for Aquarius called *Walking Through Fire* in 1985. The trademark three-guitar attack and monster rhythm section were replaced by layers of synthesizers and triggered drums.

The classic lineup of Myles Goodwyn, Jerry Mercer, Gary Moffet, Steve Lang, and Brian Greenway really only made four albums together, *First Glance, Harder... Faster, Nature of the Beast*, and *Powerplay*. The 1977 *Forever for Now* was essentially a Myles solo album and, at the end of the day, so was *Animal Grace*. Even if you believe Myles Goodwyn *was* April Wine, he's best remembered for the four albums he made with the others.

When the JUNO committee inducted April Wine into the Canadian Music Hall of Fame in 2010, it was a case of finally giving credit where it was due. Unfortunately, an opportunity to put past differences aside for even just one day was missed. April Wine's music has aged very well. But for some of those who made the music the taste of wine was not so sweet.

CHAPTER SEVEN

THE SHIT-SHOWS

THINGS GO WRONG ON EVERY tour. It's inevitable, even if what goes wrong is entirely avoidable. However, some shows are particularly odd. If nothing seemed to go right or an audience was in a strange mood, we would refer to these as "Full Moon shows".

Over the many years I experienced my fair share of "Full Moon shows." Some were exasperating, and some were funny in retrospect. And some were shit-shows.

THE TRIBE

The Simmons Rink in Saint John, New Brunswick, was in a rough neighbourhood in a city already well-known for its mean streak. We had a show with The Stampeders where just about everything that happened was screwed up.

A year earlier, I had a run-in with a motorcycle club called the Thirteenth Tribe. I tried to intervene when some bikers decided to reserve the first two rows at an April Wine concert in the Capitol Theatre. Fortunately, their leader Chico stepped in and we negotiated a compromise. They would let the kids have at least some of the seats and in exchange, I would do a shout-out to the Tribe when I introduced the band.

This year, the Thirteenth Tribe was back and it seemed some of the younger members wanted to impress Chico by raising a little hell.

Shortly after our opening act Thundermug hit the stage, there was a loud crash outside. I went to check and found that someone had tried to drive an old Ford through the loading door. Presumably, this was an attempt to enter the concert without paying but fortunately, the driver smashed into the door frame, braining himself in the process.

While I was on the phone to the police, I was told that some guys were stealing the box office; not the box office receipts, but the entire box office. The Simmons Rink provided us with a small wooden ticket booth. Claire Giroux ran the D.K.D. office but would sometimes be on tour with me. On this tour, she was managing the money. By the time I got to the front of the building, four guys were carrying the ticket booth out the front door with Claire still inside. I yelled at them to set the booth down. Fortunately, a police cruiser, responding to the loading door incident, was fast-approaching with sirens blaring. The thieves dropped the box office and scattered.

Just then, Ian Dunbar told me I had to see what had happened behind the stage. The back of the stage was blocked off from the arena wall by a black wooden scrim. Someone had snuck between the scrim and the wall with a pair of tin shears and cut three new entrances into the aluminum siding of the arena. One would have done the trick. Three was just fucking with us.

I went to the dressing room, filled a pail with cold beers and went back into the hall to look for Chico. He seemed to be expecting me. I handed him the bucket of beer and said, "Here you go, Chico. You win."

I walked past stage as Thundermug was on their last song, a real rouser called "Africa." Kids in the audience were going wild, jumping up and down with reckless abandon, *to the kazoo solo*. This evening was absurd.

SLIPPERY WHEN FROZEN

At a show in Saskatchewan, the arena manager cheaped-out. Instead of using plywood to cover the hockey rink ice, he used green polyurethane. This was the same material used to make garbage bags, only a little bit thicker. It may have been cheaper than plywood, but it had one huge drawback. When you put a plastic sheet on top of the ice and then try to walk on it, you will fall down. Maybe not right away, but you *are going to* fall down.

After the first dozen or so paying customers landed heavily on their asses, some hitting their heads, we knew we had a serious problem. As funny as it can be to see somebody slip, stumble and wipe out, over and over again, it was getting grim. If The Stampeders had drawn senior citizens instead of teenagers, there might have been an actual death toll. Though the teens would usually be front and centre by the stage, we forced them to remain in the stands. The show at the Prince Albert Communiplex went from being a rock concert to a recital.

YARMOUTH, NS

I had never played a show in Yarmouth, Nova Scotia, population 7,200. The town is at the southern tip of the province and en route to nowhere unless you were planning to catch a ferry, which in those days went to Bar Harbor, Maine.

Six weeks before this Stampeders show, I drove the three and a half hours south of Halifax to meet with the arena manager and go over the details. I left him the staging and electrical specs and arranged for the loaders and box office/door staff. The arena manager assured me he was on the case. What could go wrong?

On the day of the show, I got to the rink about an hour after the crew had arrived. My first hint of trouble was the Stampeders' truck sitting, fully loaded, in the parking lot.

Luffy came up to me and said, "You aren't going to believe this place."

He was correct.

The arena floor was covered with dirt and straw and when you looked just a little closer, you could see it was sprinkled with horse dung. Apparently, we were preceded by an agricultural fair.

Then there was the stage.

The Stampeders could, and occasionally did, perform on stages as small as a wrestling ring. It was tight and required additional platforms for the P.A., but it was do-able. However, this stage, which had been positioned at centre ice, was almost half the size. Worst of all, it was only one foot high. Fortunately, Kim's drum riser was two feet high so we could set it up in the dirt behind centre-stage. It might even look cool if anyone could see it. Our solution to (hopefully) improve sightlines was to set up a barrier to keep people further back. The arena manager said he had some fencing. Great!

I helped the crew and local stagehands lift the wheeled equipment so as not to get dirt and horse-shit over everything. By the time we were set up, our barrier arrived. That too was a left-over from the fair.

What the arena manager provided were sections of miniature white picket fencing used to display small animals. It was
fifteen inches high. I didn't think it would keep Yarmouth's
youth at bay, but it was all we had.

When the staging was complete, our little island of musical
gear with its precious little white picket fence looked like a
stage for a kids' rock camp. Hopefully, The Stampeders would
appreciate the cuteness of it all.

As it turned out, Ronnie thought it was funny, Kim didn't
and Richard was philosophical to the effect that it wasn't the
worst staging he had ever seen.

On top of this, the Stampeders were cutting corners
wherever possible to keep pace with other Canadian touring
bands. They didn't have the budget for top-end professional
lighting equipment. Instead, they had police "chaser" lights
from Canadian Tire. Each light required an adjacent jerry-
rigged transformer so we could run a 12-volt DC appliance
using 110 AC.

One of the effects involved Kim using flaming mallets for
his drum solo. At the finale, he would take the (hopefully)
still-burning mallets and bash an isolated floor tom which was
soaked in what an arson squad would refer to as an "acceler-
ant." If all went right, a flame would leap up, the crowd would
be delighted, and Kim wouldn't catch fire.

As show time approached, there was another wrinkle. Joel,
the lighting director, and more importantly, electrical expert,
had severe food poisoning and was closely monitoring the
toilet back at the motel. As a result, Luffy would do double-
duty, mixing the sound and manning the adjacent lighting
console. Ian "Snake" Dunbar, who was the stage tech, would
assume Joel's task of checking the stage wiring.

The show began well enough. Luffy was running between
the lighting and soundboards like a one-man mission control

launching a rocket. He knew the musical cues so well he could do his and Joel's job without even looking at the stage.

A transformer next to the police light at centre-stage suddenly caught fire, sending flames at least a foot into the air. Kim was the first to notice and started waving his drumsticks frantically trying to point out the fire. Ronnie was too busy working the room to notice Kim, and Snake was on the other side of the stage hitting on some girl.

Finally, Kim got Richard's attention. Richard was playing his classic double-neck Gibson and on this night, he was sporting knee-high plastic boots. I don't know if he thought the plastic would insulate him or he didn't even consider this was an electrical fire, but he moved quickly and courageously to stomp out the flames.

The instant he drove his foot into the transformer, he was jolted off stage towards the audience. He landed in the dirt but managed to protect his guitar. Meanwhile, his cowboy hat went flying and landed on the little white picket fence.

The crowd erupted in cheers! I was watching from the audience and overheard two guys in front of me.

"D'ya see that!?"

"Yeah, I never thought the big fucker could move so fast!"

Snake finally made himself useful by putting out the fire with an extinguisher.

Richard wasn't hurt. In fact, he felt electrified. He and his guitar needed a little cleaning up, but he got back on stage and continued with the set. Kim ended the show with more flames, the ones that were actually planned, and the audience went nuts.

As screwed up as the entire day had been, I think we all took pride in the idea that any band playing the Yarmouth Arena after us would have a very hard time topping this show.

TISDALE, SK

It was apparent something was wrong when I arrived at the arena in Tisdale, Saskatchewan at about noon for an April Wine concert. Just like in Yarmouth, the crew was standing around in the parking lot when they should have been loading in and setting up the gear. Sure enough, the problem was evident with one look at the stage.

Like Yarmouth, the stage was placed at centre ice. Unlike Yarmouth, it was a standard thirty-by-forty foot surface which was five feet high. The problem was that it was sitting in a pond of slowly rising ice-cold water.

I thought the ice plant had failed but surprisingly, the arena manager told me he had intentionally shut it down so it wouldn't be so cold for everyone. Of course, it was just as cold but now the air was damp and the floor had an inch of water with ice underneath.

The manager offered to turn the compressor back on and by show-time, we might have either a hard surface or a huge puddle of slush. If we did manage to make ice, half the night would be spent chipping wiring and other gear out of that ice. Instead, we decided to keep the compressor off and let the show go on. We should have cancelled.

We built bridges so the stage could be accessible while keeping the gear dry. Meanwhile, the local rink rats set out chairs in the deepening water; we were expecting a larger crowd than the seating in the stands could handle, and nobody could stand in that ice-cold pond.

At soundcheck, we discovered we would have to accept two issues; the P.A. would feature a loud buzzing sound, and the microphones would give you a little shock if you touched them and a much bigger shock if you touched them while also touching an electric instrument. Jimmy Clench had done just that. Afterwards, he complained his front teeth felt loose. Our fix was to tape cardboard cylinders to all the mics so that nobody accidentally "kissed" one of them.

Reckless Eddy opened that night. I remember the audience before me sitting cross-legged on top of the metal chairs. Vapour came out of my mouth every time I exhaled and each guitar string went out of tune at a different rate. With my mind on autopilot, I channeled an old Anne Murray gag where she asked the audience, on the count of three, to shake hands with the person on their left. Of course, nobody would be facing each other to shake hands. I thought it would be funnier for everyone to give the person on their left a friendly little punch on the shoulder. However, I didn't expect them to knock each other into the freezing water. This wasn't my finest hour.

After the show, April Wine planned on going straight back to a day-room Lloyd had booked at a nearby motel. The hope was they could get the cold and damp out of their clothes, if not their bones, before we were on the road to Prince Albert.

We arrived back at the room and turned the heater on high. A couple of cars pulled into the spaces just outside the window. It was a delegation of local heads who wanted to offer a tribute to April Wine in thanks for coming to this "god-forsaken corner of the world" (their words, not mine). Their tribute consisted of what they called "Tisdale Green" which they admitted was crappy grass. One of them optimistically suggested it would take a couple of joints for one person to get a buzz. They had at least a dozen of pre-rolled joints and proceeded to fire up a few.

Then a second delegation arrived. One of the local hippies parted the curtains and loudly told the room, "It's the man!" Our long-haired guests fled. This new delegation arrived in R.C.M.P. cruisers but they didn't have a search warrant.

Instead, they were holding a plaque from a local service group called The Kinsmen honouring April Wine for visiting Tisdale. However, with the unmistakable scent of Tisdale green in the air, the group of local business leaders and cops quickly left.

When we were all in Prince Albert a couple hours later, the band agreed we should be careful about any drugs we might be holding. I collected all of the musicians' smoke and our soundman said he could find a good place to stash it.

Sure enough, at eleven a.m. the next morning, a raiding party of at least a dozen cops hit the motel. By then, the crew was already at the venue loading in so April Wine, Lloyd, and I watched the rooms get tossed and luggage searched. Of course, they turned up nothing and by two p.m., the police left. I made my way over to the rec centre where the show was setting up and updated the crew. The soundman told me the drugs were inside one of the top P.A. cabinets in the stacks. Unless their dogs could climb ladders, we should be fine.

At about six-thirty that evening, the cops raided the venue. They interrupted our set-up and told the crew to stop what they were doing. Our intrepid soundman told the police he had to prepare for a show; they were free to watch so long as they didn't try to help. And so the cops began searching through cases and poking around all the stage gear. One of them wanted to see inside one of the P.A. speakers. Our soundman knew exactly which one had the drugs so he started dramatically ripping grills off the other speakers while ranting, "You want me to start removing the speakers!? Are you gonna refund the tickets when there's no show tonight?"

That was my cue. I opened the doors and started admitting the audience. The lead officer came at me saying he didn't say I could open the doors. I told him he never said I couldn't and our advertising stated doors open at seven. Several hundred kids started pouring into the room.

Once again, the Horsemen had been thwarted. I figured we were out of the woods but I was wrong. The next morning, as our station wagons were pulling out of the motel parking lot, the police hit us again. The same commanding officer had been running this three-act farce. But it seemed like a different cast of constables each time. I was no longer hiding my impatience and asked, "What are you running here, some kind of school for narcs?"

He smiled, "Exactly."

It turned out Prince Albert was where the R.C.M.P. had narcotics training for the recruits. I was actually surprised but pressed on, "So? What gives you the right to practice on April Wine?"

Still smiling, he said, "Tisdale."

That's when it hit me. The two delegations which showed up at the motel in Tisdale had to be pre-arranged by the R.C.M.P. For that matter, they may have even come up with the idea of turning off the ice plant. We only booked the motel room on the day of the show because the band couldn't hang out in the damp and cold arena. How did two very distinct groups of people make elaborate plans to visit that motel room after the show? We couldn't be busted in Tisdale since that useless pot had clearly been foisted upon us. But because of Tisdale, April Wine could be used as training for novice narcs.

Even if this conspiracy theory didn't have any merit, somebody certainly went to a good deal of trouble to set us up and we were lucky to emerge unscathed. What saved us were the same factors which made it possible to spend months working sixteen-hour days while traversing five time zones. We trusted each other and we shared information. If the R.C.M.P. were a team, so were we.

PURPLE DRANK

One of my early experiences with April Wine was a show in Halifax's Capital Theatre on the 1972 tour. This was to be April Wine's triumphant homecoming. But Myles was suffering from a bad cold and sore throat. He didn't realize his remedy of choice, Benadryl, was an intoxicant known on the street as "Purple Drank."

What he did know was, as the show went on, the stuff was working. Not only was his voice holding up, but his mood improved with every swig from the family-size bottle of cough medicine. Myles got through the entire show and encore before passing out backstage. He would always take justifiable pride in the fact, no matter how shitty he was feeling, the show would go on.

JAILBREAK

The next time April Wine toured in the Maritimes, I was a full-fledged tour manager. By then, the group were celebrities in parts of Atlantic Canada. They were even invited for drinks by the premier of New Brunswick, Richard Hatfield, at his residence. But what I remember best about that tour was a night-off in Moncton when we spent the evening at a club in Highfield Square. People seemed to be waiting in line to buy drinks for the band members and Myles, in particular, was flying by last-call.

On the drive back to the motel, Myles started yelling to stop the car so he could have a piss. When we did, he ran off in the direction of a large building we had just passed. It turns out it was nurses' residence. He somehow got inside the place but by the time we caught up to him, he was being escorted out.

Back in the car heading up Mountain Road, Myles spotted Deluxe French Fries and started yelling again for us to stop. This actually didn't seem like such a bad idea. While we waited for our take-out order Myles spent the whole time trying to chat up some girls sitting with their clearly pissed-off boyfriends.

When we finally made it to the Wandlyn Motor Hotel at Magnetic Hill, it was time for a joint. A few minutes later, someone asked where Myles had gone. My rental car was missing and I thought aloud, "I didn't know Myles knew how to drive."

The band's road manager, Lloyd Brault admitted he didn't either but added, "I *know* he doesn't have a driver's license."

This wasn't good. Myles was D.U.I. somewhere in Moncton. In the back of the station wagon was a case of cheap wine which had "April Wine" labels stuck on the bottles. David Henman suggested we call the police but nobody thought this was a good idea. Instead, if Myles wasn't back by morning we would try checking the hospitals.

The following day, Myles still hadn't shown up. We waited as long as we could before we headed off to the next gig in Amherst, Nova Scotia. Once there, I made my rounds getting dressing room supplies, closing down advance sale outlets, and checking out the arena before heading back to the motel to find out if there would even be a show.

The band, minus Myles, was at swimming pool. I wondered how long I should wait before telling the radio station the show was cancelled. Just then, Myles straggled in looking like he'd fallen off a boat and washed ashore.

He told us that after he got into the car, he realized he was hungry. By the time he got into town, the only place open was a greasy spoon at the Dieppe-end of Main Street. He sat waiting for his food for so long, he was getting upset. After the food was served, he started loudly complaining about how it was crap. The chef came out from the kitchen to confront Myles, but somebody jumped up and decked the chef. Myles and this other customer beat a hasty retreat and were soon cruising around Moncton. It turned out this guy had just been released from the federal penitentiary at Dorchester.

The ex-con suggested they stop by this brothel he knew. However, when they got there, the madam told them she had retired a long time ago and the business was closed. Makes you wonder how long that guy had been in prison. But Myles revealed he had a full case of wine, so a few phone calls went out and a hastily organized party was soon in full swing.

Twelve hours later, Myles somehow made it to the motel in Amherst. He probably didn't get much sleep and definitely needed a shower. But what could have been an absolute shitshow turned out to be just another night at the rink.

MAC'S PARTY

Jerry Mercer and Gary Moffet made their debut with April Wine on Labour Day weekend 1973. I wasn't able to see their first show opening for Three Dog Night and T-Rex at the Canadian National Exhibition's Grandstand in Toronto. But I did catch parts of their second show because I was on loan from D.K.D. as the stage manager at a festival in upstate Vermont called Mac's Party.

The headline acts were Mahogany Rush on Friday and April Wine on Saturday. About eight other bands were performing each day, half from Canada and half from New

England. We had about six thousand paying customers and a quarter that number outside the fences where they could barely see the stage. Patrolling the perimeter was a motor-cycle club from Connecticut called The Devil's Disciples.

A couple of announcers from the presenting radio station were emceeing. One of them got this idea between sets on Saturday afternoon to hold a "Beautiful Tits Contest." I thought it would never work. But in a matter of minutes four women were on stage ready to compete. On the count of three it was, "Tee-shirts off!" The audience cheered as each contestant, in turn, bounced up and down. The winner was the girl who got the loudest cheers.

"So, what's my prize?" she asked.

Our professional radio announcer thought quickly, "A six-pack of beer!"

"Oh shit, I want something better than that," she replied.

"Like what?"

Without hesitating, she said, "I think we should have a Beautiful Cock Contest, and I wanna be the judge."

Some women in the audience applauded but the announcer half-joked we could all wind up in jail. He told her she was welcome to have her Beautiful Cock Contest, but she'd have to do it back-stage.

Later in the afternoon, Donald and Terry came to check out the new April Wine. They were at the gate of the parking compound so I went over to let them through. As we walked through the parking area, we noticed a couple between two trucks, screwing on the grass. It was Miss Beautiful Tits and, I assumed, the winner of her Beautiful Cock contest.

Terry and I kept walking, but Donald stopped in his tracks. "Come on Donald, leave them alone. They're contest winners," I said. But he was transfixed. He slowly approached them, like an amorous zombie. When he got within a few feet, the girl noticed.

"Time out, time out!" Tapping the guy on top of her, she yelled at Donald, "Hey, this ain't no gang bang… Fuck off!" Donald, like a naughty schoolboy caught in the girls' washroom, scurried back to us chuckling.

By the time April Wine went on stage, The Devil's Disciples had been taking abuse from the people outside the fences for about thirty hours. This was coming to a head. After nightfall, people began throwing things at them. One of the bikers fired a shotgun in the air and tore open the fences to let the crowd in. A few minutes later, a delegation of Disciples was backstage, demanding to make an announcement to the crowd. However, they would have to fight their way past Terry who, like Horatio on the Bridge, was defending the one narrow ramp leading onto the stage. He made it clear they had to wait until his band finished. Surprisingly, they waited.

After April Wine's set, the Disciples went on stage and addressed the crowd. They delivered a profanity-laced warning to all the people who had been screwing with them for the past day and a half. They knew who they were and intended to settle some scores.

The smart gate-crashers quickly left. The following morning, The Devil's Disciples scoured the festival site. Whenever they identified "one of them", there was a beating ending with someone being tossed into a dumpster.

CHAPTER EIGHT

THE BEE GEES

THE GIBB BROTHERS HAD A string of hits between 1967 and 1969 but then, just as the arena rock scene was exploding, Robin left. Later that year, Barry and Maurice decided to call it quits. In 1970, they got back together and at first it seemed like nothing had changed. They recorded two of their biggest hits, "Lonely Days, Lonely Nights" and "How Can You Mend a Broken Heart?" But over the next few years, the Bee Gees experienced a prolonged dry spell.

I did two tours with the Bee Gees. The first was in 1974 during this dry spell, and the other in 1975 right when it ended and the band was about to rise from stardom to super-stardom.

THE DRY SPELL

The first tour only covered The Maritimes and Montreal. Their latest album was *Mister Natural*, produced by Arif Mardin. An urban influence was emerging and the album had some good songs, but in terms of hits, the Bee Gees were still in the wilderness. Even the radio stations presenting the tour wouldn't play the recent recordings.

General morale on this tour was good mainly because of Barry Gibb and his wife, Linda. He may have been a heart-throb and she was an actual beauty queen, but they were two of the most down-to-earth and straight-forward people you could ever meet. They seemed to go out of their way to make everyone on the tour feel appreciated. But the twins, Maurice and Robin were another story.

Maurice was going through the late stages of a messy and drawn-out breakup with his wife, the English pop-star/actress Lulu. The English tabloids feasted on story, making a painful experience much worse. Maurice's alcohol abuse was publicly cited as their main problem. Not surprisingly, he dealt with his dilemma by drinking. Early in the day he might be laughing and joking but as the hours wore on, it became obvious that Maurice Gibb was deeply unhappy.

Meanwhile, Robin seemed convinced the future of the band lay in the past when they were making *serious* albums like *Odessa* and *Trafalgar.* Maybe he thought the Bee Gees should take a cue from Al Stewart and hit the history books for inspiration. After all, the song which launched the band in North America was "New York Mining Disaster 1941." One thing was for sure, Robin Gibb in 1974 was the last person you would see at the vanguard of a disco explosion.

The Bee Gees had loyal and loving fans wherever they went. However, for this first tour in 1974, there simply didn't seem to be enough of them. What a difference a year made.

THE CELEBRATION TOUR

In 1975, Arif Mardin completed his transformation of the Bee Gees' sound when he produced the *Main Course* album. It featured three Top Ten hits. Besides "Jive Talkin'", there was "Nights on Broadway" and "Fanny (Be Tender with My

Love)." Barry liked to point out there could have been a fourth hit if Polydor hadn't made one of the best songs, "Wind of Change", the B-side of "Jive Talkin'" over his objections. But more than just returning to the charts, the Bee Gees now had a sound the world would embrace.

This time, their cross-Canada tour would be a month-long celebration. However, we almost didn't get the dates.

The Bee Gees were managed by Robert Stigwood whose R.S.O. Records was also the band's label. But The Robert Stigwood Organization was large and diverse; involved in tours, stage plays, movies, and television productions. So the effective manager of The Bee Gees was R.S.O.'s Dick Ashby.

In early 1975, Donald was locked in a competition with Michael Cohl at Concert Productions International in Toronto to get the next Bee Gees Canadian tour. Dick Ashby informed Donald and Michael he wouldn't choose between them. If they refused to join forces and work together, he would give the entire tour to "The Two Garys" (a Toronto company run by Gary Topp and Gary Cormier). From Donald's perspective, I can tell you Michael Cohl was "the enemy." I wouldn't be surprised if Michael was equally unenthused about the idea of working with Donald. However, The Bee Gees forced them to get along.

On the surface, Donald and Michael were polar opposites. Donald was large, loud, and pretty much the archetypal W.A.S.P. Michael was slender, understated, and Jewish. Donald's fashion sense might be inspired by Paul Anka. Michael looked like a keyboard player for the Grateful Dead. Donald drove a new Cadillac. Michael drove an old Volkswagen. Yet as soon as they started speaking about Bee Gees business, they discovered they were kindred spirits. They both enjoyed music, golf, sports betting, and structuring deals. When the tour began, Donald and Michael were both on hand to keep an eye on each other. But by the third show (in Kamloops), they were off playing eighteen holes. When they rolled into the venue that evening, it was obvious to everyone a bromance was in bloom. This would turn out to be a lifelong friendship. The most significant partnership in the history of Canada's concert business might never have happened if not for Dick Ashby and The Bee Gees.

Before I headed out to the first 1975 show in Victoria, the head of promotion at Polydor (R.S.O. Record's Canadian distributor) gave me an ounce of Afghani hash which was a gift for Barry. When I got to the Empress Hotel, I rang him up and told him I had a gift from his record company. However, when I showed Barry and Linda the large chunk of hash, they seemed disappointed.

"I can't smoke this stuff. It will knock me on my ass", he explained. "I like pot, the weaker the better, mixed in with tobacco. I just like to take the edge off."

Well in that case, I had some great news for them. Before leaving Montreal, I had only been able to score Mexican "brick" for myself. This was stuff that had been compressed into bricks and was so powdery you had to mix it with tobacco or smoke it in a pipe. It was shit. I told Barry I'd be getting some good pot for myself, probably in Vancouver and he was more than welcome to my stash. He suggested we "just trade." I explained his hash was worth at least three-hundred bucks and my lid of pot was a rip-off at twenty.

"Oh, I don't care about that", Barry said, "But if it makes you feel better, roll a big spliff for Tommy (the Bee Gees' stage manager) every day at tea time."

I could tell this was going to be a fun tour.

Right from the get-go, I noticed the twins were in much better spirits. Maurice was with a woman named Yvonne. They would marry once the tour was over. His "happiness act" wasn't an act anymore. Robin was still perplexed about the musical direction of the band. He still wasn't sold on the idea of dance music or all that falsetto, but he was excited the Bee Gees were back on top. "Jive Talkin" was a #1 hit in Canada and the U.S. and opened the door to a remarkable string of hits.

On this tour, the band was outstanding. Keyboardist Blue Weaver, guitarist Alan Kendall, and drummer Dennis Bryon were the core of a band; not just sidemen. Blue doubled many of Maurice's bass parts on synth so the songs had much more "bounce." Meanwhile, several of the players in the horn section would go on to gain semi-fame in Howard Shore and The All-Nurse Band on Saturday Night Live.

HEART

Even the opening act on the Western dates of that tour was stellar. I believe Heart's music was initially underrated because so much attention focused on Ann and Nancy Wilson's looks. Sure, they were beautiful women. But appearances aside, both were great song writers, Annie's voice was a natural wonder, and Nancy was a very good guitarist who could also easily handle lead vocals (listen to "These Dreams"). The Bee Gees made a point of getting to the rinks early enough to catch their set and would sometimes invite Ann to join them in their vocal warm-ups.

Before their debut album, *Dreamboat Annie* was released, Shelly Siegel, the creative director of Mushroom Records, came to Aquarius and played the album for us. He was interested in partnering on the release. Terry and I thought it sounded like there were a couple of songs that would get airplay. However, Lloyd Brault suggested a rock band fronted by two beautiful women might not be taken seriously. Bob Rags agreed with Lloyd and Donald sided with the nays.

If Aquarius had released *Dreamboat Annie* in Canada, it would have been the biggest hit in the label's history. Not only did the album produce three hit singles, but every track was a keeper. *Dreamboat Annie* entered the Top 10 of Billboard's Album Chart in two different years, which must be some kind of record.

WRAP UP

The final weekend of the tour had to be rescheduled. There was an accident involving one of the trucks and though nobody was hurt, the Moncton show was moved from a Friday night to a Sunday afternoon.

With the band flying out that evening, Barry put out a post-concert call to the band and crew to come to his room for a little party. Once we assembled, Barry took out a shopping bag full of combustible gifts that fans had given to the band as they made their way across the country. Our challenge was to smoke it all before heading to the airport. After an hour of huffing and puffing, we all had red eyes and smelly clothes but still hadn't put a dent in the stash.

Airport security must have smelled the pot, and it's not as if any of us were behaving normally (except maybe Robin). However, as I said earlier, police are very nice to artists who are well-liked by the officers' wives, sisters, and moms. The Bee Gees certainly had that going for them. This was easily one of the most enjoyable tours I ever worked and as a parting gift, Barry gave me the shopping bag of weed we had been unable to smoke.

CHAPTER NINE

RUSH AND MR MOON

CANADIAN FM RADIO FIRST EMBRACED Rush in 1975 with the release of "Fly by Night." Some Top 40 stations even played an earlier single called "In the Mood (Quarter to Eight)." However, Rush wasn't famous for their singles. They became one of the most famous Canadian bands in the world because of their albums and live show. Their 1976 "All the World's a Stage Tour" included a Canadian segment that would take them through every province, except Newfoundland, in thirty days. I got to work these dates.

THE CREW

From day-one, it was evident the Rush crew was dedicated, confident, and had great morale. A crew is usually a reflection of their band and it came as no surprise to find the guys in the band inspired all of these things. They made a point of eating the crew meal knowing that promoters would likely provide better food if the three guys in Rush would be eating it. The band would even stay at the venue from soundcheck right through until the load-out. They also had a policy where core crew members would rotate in as a "band-member for a day." This meant each crew-member would have a regular turn at traveling on the band bus and working a considerably shorter day.

Rush's dressing room rider was typical for that period. It included beer, wine, and lots of high-end liquor. Though Alex Lifeson seemed to like his beverages more than Geddy Lee or Neil Peart, neither the band nor the crew were big drinkers. Most days did not end with a party. By the end of a tour cycle, Rush would have amassed enough booze to stock a small liquor store. The band made a point of giving it all to the crew.

Another example of Rush's thoughtfulness was the deal they had with their road manager, Howard "Hearns" Ungerleider. Howard was a New Yorker who, as an adolescent, haunted Bill Graham's Fillmore East. Apparently, the people at the Fillmore gave up on trying to keep young Howard out of the building, so they allowed him to "do his thing" in return for working as a runner. Howard's "thing" was stage lighting. Howard would make notes and diagrams of the lighting used for every show at the Fillmore East. While still in his teens, he became as knowledgeable as most of the lighting directors in the rock music business.

Howard convinced Rush, rather than leasing the lighting for each year's tour, they should provide him with what they budgeted for lighting. That way, he could purchase some of the lighting equipment used in Rush's shows. From the start, Howard was able to provide a state-of-the-art customized light system and each year, it got upgraded. He still needed to rent what he couldn't afford to buy, but the cost to Rush was never more than the budget for leased lighting. Howard was a brilliant lighting designer and because the band enabled him to realize his vision, he made sure that whatever he came up with was in a class by itself. When the band wasn't touring, Howard rented his lights to other companies.

The guys who worked on the road for Rush took pride in their abilities and their great employers. This can be critical to not only a show going well, but to keeping the band and the audience safe.

The fifty-something-year-old Halifax Forum was made entirely of wood and stood on piers. It had always seemed to me that if a fire broke out, the entire building would have gone up like kindling. When the house lights went down and Rush took the stage, some people in the crowd lit sparklers and tossed them into the air. At least one of the sparklers landed on top of the large cubic score-clock suspended over centre ice. A few minutes later, flames were leaping up. Geddy spotted the fire and immediately signalled for the band to stop playing. He called out "crew, crew, crew…" while pointing to the flames.

The Rush crew sprang into action as if they were executing a well-practiced drill. Security Chief Mike Lurch who, at 6' 10", was an imposing figure, cleared a path through the crowd. Right behind him, two crew members were pushing a "cherry picker" (a wheeled ladder used for aiming lights) while another crew member was already scrambling up the ladder with a fire extinguisher. Within ninety seconds of Geddy spotting the flames, the fire was out. A second fire extinguisher was emptied onto the score-clock just for good measure and a couple of minutes later, the show resumed.

At the end of the night, the arena manager, Keith Lewis, asked me to take him to the band. He had a 128-ounce bottle of rum in each arm. The manager said Rush and their crew had prevented a disaster and if he had a million dollars, he would give it to them. "But I've only got these two bottles to offer you as thanks." There were tears in his eyes.

DEAN'S M-80S

Thanks to the successful collaboration with the Bee Gees, D.K.D. started partnering with Michael Cohl's Concert Productions International (C.P.I.) on all Canadian tours other than April Wine and The Stampeders. C.P.I. had good tour managers except for the one they assigned us for this tour: Dean.

Dean was new to touring and I quickly learned that he was pretty much useless. He had zero experience and much of the time, was simply absent. If ever he was around and was asked to help with something, he'd say he couldn't since he had to carry his briefcase full of tour files with him all the time. His other hand was usually holding a coffee cup. The Rush crew quickly learned Dean's default response to any request was to refer them to me.

Rush's show was the first tour I worked that needed four spotlights instead of the usual two. About half of the arenas we played couldn't provide all the spotlights they needed, so I got two extra lights which traveled with the Rush gear, and brought along Kenny Brault. He had plenty of experience running a spotlight at April Wine's shows. He, in turn, recruited a friend named Kim Sorrette to be the other spot operator. For the venues that had adequate equipment and personnel, Kenny and Kim would have the night off and happily spent their time drinking.

While most of us simply ignored Dean, Kenny developed a very bad attitude towards him. Normally it didn't amount to more than casting shade, but it got meaner if he had been drinking. For our show at the Brandon Sportsplex, Kenny and Kim had the night off and the two light operators got lit.

After the concert, we checked into the motel. When we got to the front desk, Dean made a point of saying that he wanted his room to be as far away as possible from "these ass-holes", indicating me, Kenny, and Kim. The two-storey motel had an enclosed central swimming pool with surrounding walkway on the second floor. Our room was on the second floor and Dean's was on the ground floor, diagonally opposite us on the other side of the pool, literally as far from "the assholes" as he could be.

On our way up to the room, Kenny spotted Dean below. He was standing still, gazing into the water. Grabbing a hanging plant, Kenny yelled, "Hey Dean, catch!" and tossed the planter towards him. Dean turned just in time and ducked out of the way. The plant landed in the pool with a large splash.

Within a few minutes, the night manager was at our door asking why we had thrown a plant into the swimming pool. Kenny demanded, "Who said we did?" hoping the manager would rat out Dean. Instead, the manager held out a key to our room. Kenny had dropped it when he threw the plant. Miraculously, we weren't kicked out right then although it might have been better if we were.

Later that evening, Kenny looked out the window and saw Dean sitting on his bed. Kenny dialed his room and when Dean answered, he hung up. This happened several times. At one point, Dean decided to take his phone off the hook but after a few minutes, put the handset back in the cradle. Kenny resumed his crank calls.

In between calls, our phone rang. It was Dean. "That's it!" he yelled. "Call me one more time, and I use the M-80s!" He slammed down the phone.

Besides his precious tour files, Dean was especially proud of some M-80s that were given to him, supposedly for out-standing service, by none other than Gene Simmons. More likely, Kiss had M-80s left over from a show in Toronto and, realizing they couldn't take them through U.S. Customs, abandoned them. Dean was always boasting about his M-80s which, I would learn, are serious firecrackers.

I told Kenny that he should knock it off or Dean might do something crazy. Sure enough, Kenny didn't, and Dean did. After one last crank call, we heard a small bomb explode just as it hit the water, causing a spectacular splash. Since the pool area was enclosed, the sound was deafening.

Soon, there were police from the City of Brandon, the local R.C.M.P. detachment, and the Canadian Pacific Railway security (C.P. was the parent company of the hotel chain). Naturally, Kenny was the chief suspect but he somehow talked his way out of being arrested. Meanwhile, Dean wasn't even identified. Lucky for him, since they would likely have found his remaining M-80s.

The next morning, the crew was leaving early because that day's show was a good four hours away in Regina. We called Dean to wake him up but his phone was off the hook. When we knocked on his door, there was no answer. I decided we had no choice but to leave without him.

The band's bus arrived at the venue in the afternoon. Dean came out first, charging towards me with his briefcase in one hand and shaking a fist with the other. Following right behind was guitarist Alex Lifeson, imitating Dean but looking more like a blonde John Cleese.

"Don't you ever leave me behind!" yelled Dean.

Alex echoed in mock fury, "Yeah, don't you ever leave this guy behind. Never. Ever. Again!"

Howard, the band's road manager, later pulled me aside and said, "Seriously, the band doesn't want Dean on our bus. Next time we'll call him a cab and you'll be paying."

After the tour, I heard Dean was fired. I encountered him a year or two later where he was staging a one-man demonstration in a parking lot outside the gates of Canada's Wonderland. He was wearing a sandwich board sign that read "Nederlander Organization Unfair to Canadian Workers." I assumed Dean was the "mistreated" Canadian worker although I'm not sure if I ever saw him actually working.

MAX WEBSTER

The opening acts on the tour were all from Rush's label and management company Anthem/S.R.O. The earlier dates were with Wireless. At a couple of Northern Ontario dates it was The Ian Thomas Band. Throughout Western Canada, it was Max Webster.

Even though this was before the release of the album *High Class in Borrowed Shoes*, Max Webster's stage attire resembled that album's artwork. It looked like they had found the worst fashion ideas of the late 1960s after scouring the teen-girl section at a thrift shop.

The audience response to Max Webster varied from town to town. There were some places like Regina where their music got little to no airplay and their weirdness was not so appreciated. Then there would be others, like at the Kinsmen Fieldhouse in Edmonton, where the crowd went wild for them.

Opening for Rush is always a difficult assignment. Though their fans obviously like other kinds of music, Rush is so unique that it's never obvious what other bands might be a good choice for an opening act. However, Max Webster might have been the perfect complement. If nothing else, they were just as unique.

A year later Max Webster would release much more accessible material, including classics like "Diamonds Diamonds", "Forget That Fear of Gravity" and "On the Road." Much later, Kim Mitchell, the singer and guitarist, would go onto have a remarkable solo career. However, in 1976, not everyone saw it coming.

MR. MOON

Rush and their crew always had very exacting standards. There was only one day off on the entire schedule and I was looking forward to a full day with nothing to do.

However, the day before my day off, I got a phone call from Donald telling me I had to work a show at the Winnipeg Arena out at Polo Park. I almost started to complain, but Donald quickly told me it was a concert by The Who.

My task was to look after the backstage area, coordinating security and dressing room riders. I had done this for shows at the Montreal Forum many times. So when The Who finally hit the stage and began performing, I decided to lie down on top of a pile of plywood in a backstage corridor.

Norman Perry, who I knew from the very early days at D.K.D. but was now Donald's west coast production partner, walked by and asked if I was alright. I was; just a little tired. He asked if I had ever seen The Who's laser show. When I said no, he said to follow him because he had the best seats in the house. The next thing I knew, I was sitting beside Norman on an amp case, directly behind Keith Moon's drum riser. During the "See me, Feel me" refrain, a bank of coloured laser beams appeared with each new lyrical phrase. These beams multiplied and when they began swirling, the air came alive. We really did have the best seats in the house.

After the show, I went back to my perch on the pile of plywood waiting until I could clear out the dressing rooms. A security guy exited by the staff door. When he opened it, there was ruckus.

The Who's bassist, John Entwistle, was walking by at that moment and asked me, "What's that all about?"

I explained there were twenty or thirty kids outside waiting for The Who to leave by the Employee's Entrance. "Except you'll be leaving in cars on the other side of the building," I added.

John asked if everything was still set up for a "meet n greet" event we had cancelled earlier. I pointed to a door nearby and told him to have a look. He took a peek and saw snacks laid out, still covered in Saran Wrap, and drinks still in ice coolers.

"Tell you what," he said. "You get those kids into this room, and I'll bring the band around in fifteen minutes."

Soon the room was filled with young Who fans eating cheese and crackers while drinking beer and wine. Some were too young to be drinking and looked like they were already having a pretty special time. I started wondering whether John was serious, but then the four members of The Who walked into the room. There was a bit of clapping but mostly stunned silence. The group took it in stride and immediately started engaging with the fans.

Bands don't always enjoy the staged fan encounters organized by radio stations or record labels. But this was spontaneous. The members of The Who seemed to be actually having a good time. I noticed Keith Moon talking to a young couple. She was about five-nine and he was over six feet; which is to say, they towered over Keith. Both were fair-haired, tanned, and radiated the image of people who might ride horses daily. Neither looked much older than seventeen.

Keith looked the girl up and down and said, "Aren't you lovely. Here, let me give you a kiss."

He swept her backwards and kissed her full on the lips. Then with a flourish, he lifted her back to her original standing position. Her date didn't know how to react; a rock idol had just kissed his girlfriend.

So Keith said, "Whatsa matter darlin'? Don't be jealous, I've got a kiss for you too!" But as he reached out to kiss the guy, the young man pushed him away.

And in that instant, Keith Moon went nuts.

A man in a suit standing in the corner of the room immediately started shouting "Band out! Band out!" He told me to get the kids out of the room immediately as he locked Keith Moon in a bear hug. The rest of us promptly cleared out. No doubt the kids would have something very cool to tell their friends.

For the next five minutes, I heard crashing from inside the "Meet 'n Greet" room, punctuated by thudding against the cinder-block walls. Finally, The Who's security man emerged from the room with Keith Moon draped over his shoulder like a sodden sleeping bag.

Three nights later in Toronto, The Who would make their next stop. It would be their last-ever, full concert appearance with Keith Moon drumming. There actually would be three more appearances with Moon, but not at a Who concert nor for a paying crowd. Keith Moon died less than two years later.

TOUR'S END

The following day, I was back with Rush and later that week we were in Saskatoon on Alex Lifeson's birthday.

As tight as the crew was with their band, the members of the band were even tighter. They were the closest of friends. Geddy and Alex were always joking around. Alex would make you laugh with his absurd, accented characters while Geddy used a much drier, observational approach. Although Neil always seemed to be buried in some serious-looking book, he was keenly aware of everything. He was the "Lifeson-Lee" comedy team's biggest fan, although he tended to let his eyes do the laughing.

That night in Saskatoon, I got pretty drunk with one of Alex's accented characters, Herr Herring. The proud Prussian was an officer in the Kaiser's army and often punctuated pronouncements by clicking his heels together. I vaguely remember lying in the back of a station wagon the next morning on the way to the show in Edmonton.

The final stop of the tour was in Victoria. Afterwards, I got Donald's blessing to stay in Vancouver for a couple of days, provided I returned the rental car in Toronto on time, and I paid for my own hotel. Since my Kenny also wanted to stay in Vancouver, it didn't cost us much to share a room at the Travelodge. We ended up staying so long, we had to drive non-stop from Vancouver to Toronto to return the car on time.

It only took us forty-five hours.

CHAPTER TEN

OTHER CANADIANS

I WORKED WITH MANY ACTS during my years at Donald K Donald Productions. Some of the talent is still world-famous, while other names are all but forgotten. Few acts used our entire national tour circuit since artists often had loyalties to regional promoters. But a year never went by when I didn't work with Canadian talent in all parts of Canada.

LIGHTHOUSE & CROWBAR

During my earliest days in the business, the two biggest Canadian bands I got to work with were Crowbar and Lighthouse. I even saw them when they were on the same bill in what developed into a "battle of the bands" at the Maple Music Junket show at Massey Hall.

Generally, the press viewed Lighthouse as a stable of thoroughbreds. Meanwhile, Crowbar was more like a team of army mules. The original Lighthouse was a thirteen-piece band with more pedigree than any two other rock bands in the country. By contrast, Hamilton's Crowbar played blues-rock with such abandon, their guitars might be out of tune before the second song of the set. But Crowbar had two things Lighthouse didn't; a true rock anthem, "Oh What a Feeling", and natural frontman, Kelly Jay.

What made this Massey Hall "battle of the bands" all the more compelling was the organizers went with the underdog, Crowbar, to close the show. Lighthouse was so insulted by being relegated to "support" status they exceeded their time allotment by 100%, claiming, in the words of drummer and spokesman Skip Prokop, "We can't get our groove together in half an hour." The Toronto reviewers would rave Lighthouse was "perfection" that night, and I can testify they were as good as I ever saw them.

But then Crowbar came on stage. Kelly Jay didn't just perform, he preached his gospel. It wasn't just a set, it was a revival meeting. The musical sermon was about how the road to rock passed through the land of the blues and the crowd was converted. The finale had an enormous multi-tiered cake wheeled on stage. As the band churned through a ten-minute version of, "Oh What a Feeling", a near-naked lady popped out of the cake and then the performers descended into the audience. Crowbar more than held their own.

I would later tour with both bands. The first time I toured with Crowbar was that time when I had just finished a Lighthouse tour and showed up at the Crowbar show half a day late with a bagful of cash. The last time I worked with Lighthouse was at the Grand Theatre in Kingston.

One of Lighthouse's great dilemmas was that they could sell out the 800-seat Grand Theatre and only break-even. With twelve or thirteen musicians and a crew of at least six or seven, Lighthouse had a lot of mouths to feed.

The group was so large it had factions. There were the vegetarians who were mocked by meat-eaters; mind you, in the early 1970s and outside of the largest cities, a meat-free diet might be limited to French fries, cheese pizzas, and coleslaw. There was also a jazz faction, a rock faction, and a faction of Bob McBride which only consisted of lead singer, Bob McBride.

Oddly, it was only during this last show when I noticed some of the band and crew didn't seem to like Bob. He would sometimes not show up for concerts. The band had enough personality and talent to play a show without him; the drummer, Skip Prokop was luminescent, Ralph Cole was an amazing guitarist and Paul Hoffert radiated the self-assurance of Buddha. With their high overhead costs, cancellation was not an option. But Bob McBride was the "rock star" of the band. It was hard to imagine Lighthouse without him. Even so, by the end of that year, Bob was fired.

It was also during this last show that I witnessed Stan the Tambourine Man's finest hour. During the load-in, a local character named Stan turned up at the stage door. Stan could be expected at most Kingston shows offering his services as a tambourine player. But this time, he was in quite a state.

"You gotta get Lighthouse outta here, right away!" he pleaded.

Apparently, someone told Stan that a Viet Cong submarine had surfaced in Kingston's harbour. Stan was on a rescue mission.

"The Viet Congs are comin'!" He insisted, "We gotta get the band outta here!"

A few years earlier, Stan had been walking along the sidewalk on Princess Street when a car climbed the curb and knocked him through a store window. The courts gave him an award which was put in a trust. This allowed Stan to pursue his career as a freelance tambourine man. Stan even invested in snappy custom-tailored purple three-piece suit.

I thanked Stan for his warning and assured him we would be ready if any "Viet Congs" showed up. I then asked the band if they would let Stan jump in with them. They obliged and Stan got to play the tambourine on stage in front of a roaring crowd that night. But only during the encore.

TRIUMPH

We were driving into Sudbury and Gil Moore and Mike Levine were explaining to me how Triumph got started. They were unemployed musicians when they had the idea of calling the two big Toronto agencies; The Agency and Music Shop. They claimed their band could do three sets of Led Zeppelin. In those days, there were lots of Elvis Presley tribute acts. But a Led Zeppelin cover band was actually a pretty novel concept. The agents quickly came back with offers. There was just one problem; there was no band.

To buy time, Gil explained they needed a continuous run of dates. So the agents went back to work and Gil and Mike began scouring the bars of the Greater Toronto Area looking for their Jimmy Page. It seems the guitar gods approved of the plan, because they managed to find guitarist Rik Emmett. Now all they needed was time to practice. Gil bought more time by explaining, since they also had Zep-inspired lighting, they would require higher guarantees. The agents got back on the phones.

Before their first performance, this completely unknown band called Triumph had over thirty well-paying gigs – all in a row. They went from being literally unknown to being one of the busiest rock bands in Toronto. Whenever I hear about any artist being an "overnight sensation" I'm always dubious. It normally takes years to "suddenly" become famous. The exception might be Triumph.

When I took them out on a tour of Northern and Eastern Ontario and the Maritimes a couple of years later, Triumph had a spectacular stage presentation. There was a formula involved. The band had gone to a Kiss concert with notepads to document every effect. Comparing notes, they came up with the stats they needed to create a show which would offer almost half of all the bells and whistles you would experience at a Kiss show. Given Kiss might have four spotlights, twenty-four explosions, a hundred par lights on trusses, and an eight-foot flame shooting out of two tubes, Triumph would have two spotlights, twelve explosions, fifty pars and a four-foot flame coming out of one tube. The one thing they didn't try to replicate was the levitating drum riser. But with all this other excitement, audiences didn't care if Gil's drum kit wasn't floating.

Usually, a rock band's crew is treated pretty equally by their employers. But the Triumph crew had a dynamic pay scale. At the top end was a lighting director they had hired away from Gino Vannelli named Peter. I knew Peter from an April Wine tour a couple of years earlier. At that time, he wasn't a lighting director; he was a truck driver. However, Peter must have had a flair for lighting, because he managed to command a wage of four hundred a week plus a twenty-five dollar per diem, all paid in U.S. dollars. At the other end of the spectrum was a pyro guy named Roach who had been with the band from the start. He worked his way up to sixty dollars a week plus ten dollars a day for food. The guy doing lights was making eight times more than the guy in charge of explosions.

We were playing the arena in Port Hawkesbury, Nova Scotia. The opening act on the tour was Teaze. Their drummer, Mike Kozak, was watching Triumph performing from a penalty box and motioned for me to come over. Pointing to the side of the stage, he said, "Can you believe it? Roach has found a lady-Roach!"

Roach was at the pyro consul at stage left and there beside him was a girl who had the same long dirty-blonde hair, the same black tee-shirt, and the same saggy "no ass" blue jeans. They looked like they might be twins.

Mike and I watched Roach point to a switch on his board and make an explosion gesture. Lady Roach pointed at the switch in a way that asked if she could flip it. Roach shook his head. Then, with a flourish, he flipped the switch himself and flash pot at the front of the stage detonated. Problem was, Roach detonated the pot without knowing what was happening on stage.

For starters, it was between songs. This was odd. But the real problem was the flash pot was right in front of Rik Emmett's pedalboard. Rik was bent over the board, adjusting some of his settings when the pot went off. The stage tech ran over to help him off stage and he was rushed to the hospital. Rik sustained burns to the side of his face, he lost of a lot of hair on that same side. Worst of all, he was (at least temporarily) deafened in one ear.

Meanwhile, the show would continue with Teaze joining Triumph for a "monster jam." I met with Gil and Mike and we agreed if anyone wanted a refund they could get one. Nobody did.

I saw Rik after the show back at the motel. His face was red and swollen, he still had ringing in one ear. To my amazement, he played the following night in Sydney.

RANDY B.T.O.

In 1975, Donald co-produced a coast-to-coast Bachman Turner Overdrive tour with Don Fox and his New Orleans-based Beaver Productions. I had encountered Randy Bachman when he was in The Guess Who. I even got to see

Brave Belt, Randy's band after The Guess Who. But I didn't get to know him until this B.T.O. tour.

After B.T.O.'s soundcheck, Randy liked to remain onstage to play with his newest toy; a tape loop. Normally, the opening act got the stage at this point. Fun as it was for us to listen to the noodling of this exceptional musician, Randy was throwing the day-of-show schedule out of whack. It looked like once again our opening act, Bob Seger and the Silver Bullet Band, wouldn't have time for a soundcheck.

It's not that Bob Seger was unknown at this point. A year earlier, B.T.O. opened for Seger. But this was just before Bob's string of hits including "Night Moves" and "Main Street". Two years later it would be hard to imagine Bob Seger opening for anyone, never mind B.T.O.

Saint John, New Brunswick, was the third show in a row where Randy was tooling around on stage with his echo machine and Seger was really pissed. I was feeling the brunt of his complaints when he spotted a better target for his anger. Walking down the hall towards us was Randy's manager, Bruce Allen, and Don Fox.

Bob Seger was half a foot shorter and 80 pounds lighter than either of them but he got right in their faces. This was "complete bullshit," he said and declared he was "outta here."

Bruce Allen, whose nickname was "The Bear", lifted Bob by the shoulders and held him against the cinderblock wall of the Lord Beaverbrook Arena. They were eye-to-eye.

"You'll leave this tour when I say you can! Understand?" growled Bruce.

Seger nodded.

Bruce set him down and said, "Go get ready for your soundcheck."

To his credit, Bruce got Randy off stage immediately and from then on, Bob Seger got all of his soundchecks.

In those days, Randy Bachman was known to be a tad judgmental. He had fired his brother, Tim, from the band a year earlier for smoking, drinking, and having sex outside of marriage. If those were firing offences in the world of rock music, I'm not sure rock would have made it into the sixties. But Randy never approved of the cliché rock and roll lifestyle.

For a Moncton show, I drove Randy out to neighbouring Amherst for a radio interview. I knew radio interviews could go wrong. The worst would have been when CFAN's Ian Buyers asked The Stampeders' Kim Berly what it felt like to be so short; Kim responded, "What does it feel like to be so fat and ugly?" This interview with Randy might have been the second-worst.

The CKDH announcer started by asking how Randy wrote all those great songs.

Randy answered, "Actually, for me it's easy. If I get a musical idea I can always tell if it's good. If I can't write a song right away, I just toss the idea into this box in my mind and at some later point come back, rummage through the box. I pull out a few ideas and put them together."

When it was time wrap things up the announcer then asked if there was anything he'd like to tell his fans in Amherst.

Randy started telling his audience not to smoke drugs or drink alcohol and that they shouldn't have sex until they were married. Then, to really slam home the point he added, "If you do those things, I'd prefer you didn't come to my concert."

Thanks, Randy. On the drive back to Moncton, we didn't talk.

Randy was always direct and unfiltered about most things. He had watched The Rolling Stones on TV and saw Mick Jagger throwing roses into the audience. Randy liked the idea and wanted to do the same, except he explained, "Roses are stupid." Randy thought they were too small to see from the back of the audience. It would be better to use carnations, "Besides, carnations are cheaper than roses."

"So, what is our budget for carnations?" I asked.

"That's the best part", Randy explained. "You can get them for free. Just go around to funeral parlours in each town and check the garbage." He was being serious.

Randy also had strict rules for promoters. One rule was each day, before soundcheck, I had to arrange all the dressing room supplies on a table for him to check each item against the receipts I provided. He would even check receipts for ice from the gas station. If a single item didn't match up, Randy would claim, "That's fraud!"

Randy's penalty for promoters who committed "fraud" was to refuse to accept the cost for *any* of the dressing room supplies at that show's settlement.

I had just finished preparing for Randy's inspection in Sydney, Nova Scotia when Donald entered the dressing room. This was another one of Donald's "visits to the front-lines."

"Look at all this tasty food," mused Donald. He reached for one of the small aluminum tubs containing Kraft cheese dip.

"No Donald, don't open it!" I said.

"Or else what?" he asked.

"Or else Randy will make you pay for all of this stuff."

Donald pulled the zip tab and removed the lid. He dipped a couple of fingers into the cheesy paste and said, "Oh yeah? Well, fuck Randy!" before shoving the dip into his mouth. He didn't realize Randy had just walked into the room.

Randy walked over to me and said, "Give me the grocery receipts."

Taking them, he turned to Donald and in the same calm voice said, "Fuck Randy?" Then he ripped the receipts to shreds and dropped them at Donald's feet. With a satisfied smile, he turned and walked out of the room.

If you met Randy's very clear expectations, you would never have a moment of grief. Like many of the successful people I've encountered (including Donald), Randy Bachman is very detail-oriented. When Randy was in The Guess Who, he and Burton Cummings were opposites. Randy had all the patience in the world and strove for perfection. Burton was a self-described "A.D.D. case." I once heard Burton say that after twenty minutes of working on writing a song, he started to lose interest. But Burton could get a lot done in twenty minutes.

The genesis of the all-time classic, "American Woman," illustrates how this odd couple complemented each other. Randy had a riff he would use to check if his guitar was properly-tuned. He was doing this onstage at a gig in Southern Ontario when bassist Jimmy Kale and drummer Gary Peterson started playing along. Burton began to ad-lib the vocal melody and lyrics. Later, they would fine-tune it, but "American Woman" took form, spontaneously, during a jam in front of a live audience at a gig in Canada.

Randy Bachman was logical and methodical; Burton Cummings was inspirational.

In 2020, Randy and Burton got together to launch a Bachman-Cummings tour. I have to think Randy insisted billing should have Bachman before Cummings. After all, it only makes sense; B comes before C in the alphabet.

THE SECRET IS DEATH

Not all of the tours I did with Canadian bands featured groups that are well-remembered. Wednesday was a band from Oshawa. Their two managers spent time in the public library studying Billboard charts, trying to figure out a way for an unknown artist to score a #1 hit. They found the answer; it was Death.

Wednesday's first three singles were covers of songs by one-hit-wonders that featured some sort of tragedy.

In "Last Kiss", star-crossed lovers swerve to miss a stalled vehicle and BAM! Our hero ends up giving his dying date a last kiss.

In "Tell Laura I Love Her" our hero competes in a stock car race so he can buy his girlfriend a ring. LOOK OUT ... CRASH! His dying words are, you guessed it; "Tell Laura I love her."

But my favourite has a couple out on a date when their car gets stuck on a train track. (I love songs about trains!) They escape, but she goes running back to fetch his school ring and..."Teen Angel."

I couldn't believe we were going to sell tickets to see a band playing this stuff on stage.

About half the shows drew hundreds of people. Others were what we referred to as "Dairy Queens" where there were just a handful of teenagers who looked like they had nothing better to do.

One of the best shows was in Sydney, Nova Scotia. The stage in the old Sydney Forum was about three feet high and the front of the stage was tightly packed with adoring fans. During one of the songs, Wednesday's lead singer, Mike O'Neil, pretended to have been shot in the heart and keeled forward into the crowd. The crowd obligingly bounced him back up onto the stage. They couldn't let their hero die.

The next show on the tour was at the French-language campus of the University of New Brunswick in Moncton; probably not the best venue to attract Wednesday's English-speaking audience of young teenage girls. This was a classic Dairy Queen.

The opening act of the tour was a weird little group called Apple Jack (not to be confused with Applejack from Vancouver which morphed into Trooper). Apple Jack included veterans of the Toronto band scene who only planned to stick with the group until something "cooler" came along. By contrast, their lead singer was a sixteen-year-old whose parents let him "live the dream" and go on his first rock tour. He saw Mike O'Neil's sick move at the last show and planned to rip it off for this one. He didn't consider this stage was two feet higher and there was nobody in front of it.

During one of the songs, Apple Jack's singer struck a rigid pose and fell like a chopped tree off the front of the stage. But unlike Mike, he didn't bounce back. Instead, the four or five girls near the stage who might have cushioned his landing, screamed and got out of the way. That was the end of their set.

Not to be outdone, Mike O'Neil found inspiration in a Mick Jagger move where Mick draped a long scarf across his neck and dangled the ends just above the audience's out-stretched hands. Simple move, but Mike missed a couple of important details. Jagger draped the scarf across the nape of his neck and made sure to keep it out of the audience's reach. Mike, meanwhile, wrapped the scarf *around* his neck and, more importantly, dangled the scarf too close.

As soon as he bent over towards the crowd, a young girl grabbed hold of the scarf and tugged *hard*. Faster than you can say "come to mama" Mike was face down on the concrete floor in almost the same spot where the Apple Jack singer had landed.

The band's road manager freaked out, ran across the stage and jumped to Mike's rescue. When he landed, he broke a leg. The good news was that Mike wasn't injured. Unlike the characters in his songs, he cheated death and even finish the show.

BROTHER AND ME

Fludd had hit songs and good albums but none of it came together in a way that would lead to their success. It wasn't as if Fludd couldn't catch a break, they just couldn't seem to string their breaks together. They never toured extensively and their music was released on three different labels. But if you compiled the ten best Fludd tracks recorded between 1971 and 1973, you would have one of the better Canadian pop/rock albums of the period.

Their first two singles, released on Warners, got them noticed. "Turned 21" was a Top 20 hit and was followed up with a pop song with a rock statement, "Get up, Get Out, Move On." Fludd then moved on to Daffodil Records and released an album which included "Always Thinking of You" and another great rock song, "C'mon C'mon." Daffodil sent them back into the studio where they recorded "I Held Out", "Dance Gypsy Dance", "Brother and Me", and another Top 20 hit, "Cousin Mary."

But even though Fludd was having the kind of radio success most bands or labels could only dream about, Daffodil didn't release another album. Instead, they licensed their four latest singles to Al Maier's Attic Records. Al used these tracks along with some new recordings to make an album entitled "Great Expectations." This album generated another hit single, "What an Animal." Yet just as it seemed like the stars were finally aligning for Fludd, in 1974 the band's lead singer and the co-writer of all their songs, Brian Pilling, was diagnosed with leukemia.

The following year, their manager convinced Donald to put Fludd on the road for their farewell tour. It would be in the Maritimes. We knew the band's profile didn't ensure strong ticket sales, so Donald bolstered the bill with a singer/

songwriter from Saint John named Kenny Tobias who, regionally at least, was probably better known than Fludd.

The first night of the tour was at the Lady Beaverbrook Arena in Fredericton. Fludd's road manager, a guy named Clay, told me whatever I was doing, I had to see the last song of the set. He promised it would be something I would never forget and showed me where to get into position for the last song. Two strings of flashbulbs were suspended from the back corners of the rink and converged to a point at the centre of the stage. At the end of the song, the bulbs flashed in sequence from back to front. It was a technically impressive, if somewhat underwhelming, effect.

When the house lights came up, Clay came towards me visibly upset. "It didn't fuckin' work. I spent two hours setting it up and it didn't fuckin' work," he spat. "Don't worry, tomorrow's gonna be great." He then stormed off to the other end of the rink where he lifted a large flash pot at centre-stage. Apparently, this was supposed to explode and be the climax of the effect.

A flash pot is a rectangular metal container with an open top. It's packed with gunpowder for the bang and magnesium for the flash. You need to run a current into it for it to explode. Normally.

Clay held up the large flash pot with both hands and slammed it down in anger. It finally went off. Clay's right hand, which was directly on top of the explosion, was badly burned. It took several hours to patch him up at the hospital, and when I drove him back to the motel, it was about four in the morning. Fludd's farewell tour was off to a terrible start.

As we worked our way through his home province of New Brunswick, Kenny Tobias was amazing. The crowds were good, his sets went off without a hitch, and it looked like the tour might even make a little money. But Brian Pilling, the singer for Fludd, was getting weaker by the show. The leukemia was taking its toll.

I discussed this with their manager, William "Skinny" Tenn, the band's lead guitarist and Brian's brother, Edmund Pilling, and his father who had just joined the tour. It seemed like this whole adventure might be too much for Brian. But we decided Brian would let us know if we had to stop. As long as he kept answering the proverbial bell, the show would go on.

We were in Charlottetown when Edmund told me Brian couldn't get out of bed. He asked if we could cancel half the dates and instead, do every second show. Maybe this was something Brian could manage, but we all knew it was over.

Brian Pilling went on to live for another three years. He would even make more recordings with his brother. Thanks to today's streaming platforms I can still listen to Fludd's music. But I know the Pilling brothers would have done so much more if they had more time.

CHAPTER ELEVEN

OFF THE ROAD

FOR NINE MONTHS OF THE year, between March and November, I would be on the road. I would do tours that introduced me to really exceptional artists like Joan Armatrading and Gentle Giant. I would tour with an Elvis impersonator who turned out to be an old high school classmate. On my first tour with Chilliwack I found them grilling hotdogs on a hibachi in their dressing room and apparently impressed them because my only concern was the danger of carbon monoxide poisoning. I would teach Blue Swede how to "shotgun" a beer.

I had incredible experiences on the road. However, if not for Montreal shows when I was off the road, I wouldn't have had the chance to score drugs for Bob Dylan or be addressed as "Sir" by Brian Wilson. Those winter months and occasional mild-weather weeks I spent in Montreal provided some of my most memorable experiences.

THE CROSSROADS

My most frequent assignment at the Forum was to look after the backstage area and see to the needs of the talent, the security, stagehands and the travelling road crews, and to know who belonged back-stage and who didn't. I tried to keep things as quiet and uneventful as possible, but it wasn't always easy.

The best place to keep track of things backstage at the Montreal Forum was to stand at "the crossroads." From there, you could see the passageway to the stage, the corridor leading to the headliner's dressing room, the entrance to the back-stage from inside the building, the backstage street-entrance, and the passage to the other side of the building where the opening act(s) and stagehands had their rooms.

The most chaotic nights were when the headliner was local and had provided All-Access passes to friends and family. At a Gino Vannelli concert, you would encounter a great many guests and it was more hectic than usual, but it was also a celebration. For me, the best shows where when a local artist finally made it big enough to play the Forum.

But it was also impressive to watch international headlin-ers being blown away by Montreal audiences. Judging from what I saw after their show, Supertramp was overwhelmed by the fan reaction the first time they headlined a sold-out Forum. The same thing happened with the debut of Styx.

A day earlier, I worked with Styx at The University of Vermont's Patrick's Gym. The band was really happy to draw about 3000 people in Burlington. Their lead singer, Dennis DeYoung, told me Styx had been a successful club act and seldom played more than a couple of hundred miles from Chicago. They were making good money but felt like they were in a rut. So, they hired a new manager, Derek Sutton.

Derek told the band they would be spending the next year on the road and probably the only place they *wouldn't* be playing was Illinois. They would also be taking a pay cut. One guitarist quit as a result, but Dennis saw the crowd in Burlington, Vermont, as a sign they might be turning a corner. He also felt their new guitarist, Tommy Shaw, added great chemistry to the band. All the other band members had attended college, but Tommy was a student of Southern rock bars.

I told Dennis he would know for sure Styx had turned a corner once they played Montreal. A big reason for all those people showing up in Burlington was the influence of Montreal's rock station; CHOM-FM. The next night they would be playing in CHOM's back-yard.

After two encores in a sold-out Montreal Forum, I caught Dennis's eye as he passed through the crossroads. His nod said it all; a dream had just come true.

Usually, bands wait to get back to the dressing room before celebrating a great performance. Supertramp and Styx were the only two times I saw the bands unable to contain their excitement as they celebrated through the crossroads. By contrast, Ian Anderson of Jethro Tull couldn't wait before ripping into his band for a list of mistakes they'd made during the first half of *Thick as a Brick*. Years later, I mentioned this to Tull guitarist Martin Barre. He laughed and said Ian had mellowed a lot since those days. At the time, it was no laughing matter.

There are some unwritten rules when working backstage. One of these is to never make eye-contact with the star of the show. Sometimes that's even written into the rider. The one time I broke this rule was after Elton John had gone back to the dressing room for a costume change. When he emerged from the corridor, he sported a stunningly colourful outfit, complete with a cape, top hat, and boots with platform soles. All of it was plastered with sequins, but what got to me was the pair of oversized glasses. I made eye contact. But then to make matters worse, I laughed. Elton would have been within his right to get someone to kick me out of the building right there and then. Instead, he gave me this look which seemed to ask, "Do I really look that daft?" I immediately felt ashamed.

Perhaps the strangest night at the crossroads involved a Beach Boys concert. The entire day had been tense and the crew was in crappy spirits right from the load-in. Apparently, Dennis Wilson and Mike Love wanted to kill each other; something to do with someone messing around with somebody's daughter. The crew clearly sympathized with Dennis, but probably because Mike Love acted like he *was* the Beach Boys. To me, this was ridiculous. As the low voice in a group that relied on harmonies, he could barely hit the notes let alone make the bass vocals resonate. I always thought if any one person was The Beach Boys it was Brian Wilson. To underline my point, the tagline for this tour was "Brian is Back."

Brian Wilson had retired from touring at the start of 1965 to concentrate on songwriting and recording. Working in his own world, Brian created the most celebrated Beach Boys album of all time, "Pet Sounds." While he was working on the follow-up album, Brian suffered a mental breakdown that would take him out of action, right at his peak. Now it was the mid-seventies and Brian is back!

From my post at the crossroads, I had a clear view of Brian's grand piano sitting at extreme stage-right. But as the show got underway, there was no Brian. A few songs into the concert, he emerged from the dressing room corridor and came over to me.

"Excuse me sir, which way is the stage?"

This was a pretty unsettling question, given the stage was brightly-lit, really loud, and about fifty feet from us. I led Brian to the stage and watched as he climbed the stairs guided by a flashlight from one of the Beach Boys' roadies.

There was loud applause from the crowd, which Brian didn't acknowledge. Instead, he tinkled on the keyboard and at the end of the song, made his way back down the stairs, came up to me and asked, "Excuse me, sir, where is the Beach Boys dressing room?"

This entire process would repeat itself two more times during the show, right down to Brian Wilson calling me "sir" each time. Clearly, it didn't seem like Brian was all the way back.

Among the many encounters at the crossroads, there was one I really didn't think much of at the time. Years later, when I was working for Aquarius, I took a meeting with a young singer named Corey Hart who was looking for a record deal. His demo included a song called "It Ain't Enough." I listened to it, and then listened again. How had he made a "demo" that was good enough to play on the radio? Who were those musicians?

He answered, "Billy Joel's band." When I asked how he managed that, he gave me the most remarkable explanation.

Corey told me that he and I had met each other a few years earlier at the crossroads before a Billy Joel concert. That afternoon, I spotted him and asked why he was backstage at the Forum. He told me he was Gerry Grundman's nephew. Gerry was the manager of the Forum. This kid had Gerry's "movie-star" good looks and lots of confidence. His story seemed credible to me, so I let him go about his business.

Turns out his business was to track down Billy's sax player, Richie Cannata and persuade him to come to a demo studio after the concert and play on a track. Why Richie actually showed up was the strangest part of the whole story.

Earlier that day, Richie's father had died. But instead of telling him, Billy Joel's manager and first wife, Elizabeth, decided it was more important to have a sax solo for "Just the Way You Are" in the show. Richie only learned about his father's death after the concert and by then, the last flight out of Montreal had already taken off. That night, Richie felt more like playing his sax than going back to an empty hotel room, and so he went to Corey's demo session.

At the end of the session, Richie told Corey he was welcome to come down to Long Island where he could work on demos to his heart's content. Sure enough, when Richie returned home after the Billy Joel tour, Corey called. Over the next eighteen months, they would make a couple of dozen very professional demos.

After I left my job as tour manager and joined Aquarius, Corey Hart signed with us. "It Ain't Enough" became a hit single in Canada and the United States.

OTHER ASSIGNMENTS

When I wasn't working the crossroads, I would draw random assignments. Once I spent a day taking The Village People around to media outlets and ended up at a party organized by their label. I had a chat with the lead singer Victor Willis, the one dressed like a cop, where he asked me to spread the word that not every "Village Person" was gay. He was frustrated that he had finally fulfilled his dream of becoming famous, and his most enthusiastic fans were men. I had a somewhat similar chat with Roger Taylor from Queen at a show in the Ottawa Civic Centre. He certainly wasn't lamenting his plight, but he commented on how few people seemed to realize only half of Queen was gay.

As part of the promotional assignments, I would take a lot of artists to radio interviews. You never quite know how they are going to go, but you always hoped for the best.

In 1972, I was assigned to take Frank Zappa to CHOM to promote a Mothers concert. I had been advised that Frank could be testy, even difficult. It didn't help that during an earlier European show, a fan attacked him on stage and he was still wearing a leg brace. The broadcast facilities at CHOM FM were on the second floor of an old Victorian house on Greene Avenue, without an elevator. I suggested we could try to run a mike down to the lobby, but Frank wasn't having it. He struggled up the long flights of stairs and to my surprise, did an interview which was both open and funny. He then struggled back down the stairs and got into the car. I couldn't have been more impressed.

Sometimes, my only, but probably most important job, was to make sure a band showed up. International border crossings tended to be an issue with rock bands because recreational drugs don't travel well. In one case, I went to a private landing strip next to Dorval airport to make sure Aerosmith got into the country. On this snowy afternoon, I found myself in a small cabin-office with the Columbia Records promo rep, Mario Lefebvre, the landing strip company guy, and a Canadian immigration officer.

The band's private jet landed and pulled up next to the building. Then it just sat there. After a few minutes, the phone rang. It was the band's road manager. He was asking for the promoter so they handed me the phone. The road manager explained the band had been "partying" and hadn't considered they were entering a foreign country. Since they were pretty stoned, they were thinking it might be better if they just flew back to the States.

I could think of several reasons why this was a terrible idea. As quietly as I could, I explained the immigration officer (who was in the room with me) only seemed to be concerned about whether he could get an autographed photo from the band. I asked if they had something they could sign for him. I could hear the road manager talking to the group. He came back on the line, sounding very relieved. "No problem, we'll be right out." Sure enough, they had an autographed glossy for the surprised, but accommodating, immigration officer. Minutes later, Aerosmith was heading downtown in a limousine.

In another drug-related incident, I was asked by Bob Dylan's road manager to score them some pot. He came up to me before the show and explained they had been afraid to bring any pot across the border. I said I'd check with some people in the venue, but if they wanted more than a couple of joints, I'd probably have to pick it up after the show and bring it back to their hotel. He was fine with that. About an hour after the show, I was in an elevator at the Chateau Champlain.

When I got off the elevator and looked for the room, I spotted a man checking to see if his hotel room door was locked. When he turned, I saw it was Bob Dylan and it was clear he thought I was a stalker. He quickly scurried down the hall. I waited a moment, and then took my time following. When he got to the door at the end of the corridor he knocked and looked back. I stopped moving, waiting until someone opened the door to let him in. A moment later, I knocked on the same door and was greeted by the smiling road manager. He invited me in. I gave him the weed and asked if he also wanted some hash – when you tell the supplier that the drugs are for Bob Dylan, they'll happily front whatever you want. I smiled at Mister Dylan and was glad to see he no longer looked stressed. As I walked back to the elevator, I was happy to think I might have helped him enjoy his time in Canada.

THE LAST GIG

My final gig for Donald turned out to be decidedly "old-school": five performances by the Bolshoi Theatre in Montreal at Place des Arts. They were staging "Swan Lake", "Romeo and Juliet" and "Electra." Barry Archer, who took me out on my first-ever tour in 1972 with April Wine, worked with me on my last set of shows.

Over 300 people were travelling with the Bolshoi. You've heard the story of the kid who played the part of a tree in the second-grade play? Some of these choristers were just that, only these kids were former Red Army and they were with one of the most celebrated touring companies on the planet.

I figured these artists came from a world where parity was the norm, but there was a stark difference between the bottom and the top of the Bolshoi's hierarchy. At the base of the pyramid were the choristers. Each day, they received their ten-dollar per diem. Many would tear off to the Woolworth's at the corner of St-Laurent and Ste-Catherine to get stylish Western clothes like the "prima" dancers wore. Of course, the top dancers had designer clothes and even their denims were from Paris and Milan. Meanwhile, our young recent-soldiers would re-enter the stage door sporting ill-fitting jeans from Romania, polyester Hawaiian shirts from Indonesia, and proud smiles. These were the real-life "Wild and Crazy Guys." They got enough catered food from us, so they spent their food-allowance on the "finer things."

We had cases of soft drinks piled next to ice coolers, enough to last through the whole engagement. But by the end of the first day, they were all gone. The choristers had stuffed their clothing and bags with all the Coke, Sprite and Fanta they could carry. The second day, we got more soda but kept the stores locked. The only cans we put out were in large pails filled with ice. Barry and I made a game of guessing who had ice-cold cans of soda under their shirts.

Another commodity we had trouble keeping in stock was toilet paper. The young Soviets couldn't get over how decadent our toilet paper was. I wondered what they would make of the pet food section of a Western supermarket. I asked one of them why they wanted to take every roll of T.P. that wasn't under lock and key. It turned out they thought our toilet paper would be the greatest gag gift ever, back in the U.S.S.R.

The prima ballerinas ranged in age. What was remarkable was the comparative size of their legs. All of the jumping around made legs get bigger, heavier and more muscled with every passing year. The youngest ballerina had the legs of a speed swimmer while the oldest dancer had the legs of a Tour de France cyclist. I knew nothing about ballet. At first, their leaps seemed unspectacular compared with figure skating I had seen on TV. Then I realized skaters are aided by velocity to get airborne. These dancers had to rely on sheer athleticism. Ballet, especially at this level, was as physically demanding as any Olympic sport.

The two stars of the Bolshoi Ballet in 1979, Alexander Godunov and Lyudmila Vlasova, were newlyweds. One afternoon, Alexander asked if I would take them for a drive around the city. I was happy to oblige. We were joined by a stocky, mean-looking 50-something woman who fit my idea of the K.G.B.

He wanted to see the most expensive neighbourhood in Montreal. I explained there might be more expensive estates on the rivers, but they were too far away and we would never be able to get close to the larger ones. However, we could be in Westmount in about ten minutes. As I drove up to Surrey Garden, the dome of Saint Joseph's Oratory came into view at the end of the street. As befitted the loftiest residential block on the island, every house is a mansion.

"How much does a house here cost?" asked Alexander.

I explained a house in Westmount recently set a record by selling for a million dollars. I suggested any of the houses on this street would cost at least that much. The K.G.B. woman riding in the back seat said something in Russian, but the word "propaganda" is universal. Clearly, she wanted Alexander to believe I was bullshitting.

"Now take me to the poorest part of Montreal." I told Alexander there might be poorer neighbourhoods further east, but if we went straight downhill towards the Saint Lawrence River it would take about ten minutes to get to St-Henri which was one of the poorer sections of Western Montreal. When we got there, our chaperone in the back seat was complaining loudly this was not a slum. I tried to explain, compared to other places where you might find entire neighbourhoods which were evidently blighted, the poorer parts of Montreal were not so apparent. Even poorer families lived in buildings that looked substantial.

Alexander pointed to a residence and asked about the price. I said it would cost about $85,000, but the building contained three large flats plus a basement unit. Now K.G.B. Lady was loudly saying "Propaganda!" over and over. During all this time Lyudmila had only said a few words in Russian. If I had to guess, she was asking Alexander to stop asking about the price of everything.

After a bit more sight-seeing and asking about the price of various cars, Alexander seemed to have all the information he needed. He showed me some movie passes and asked me to take them to the theatre. Luckily, a new multiplex just down the street from Place des Arts would honour the passes. They had a dozen or so films to choose from, except Madam

K.G.B. was putting a big "Nyet" on anything she deemed "Propaganda!" I didn't wait around to see their final selection because I was illegally parked, although my guess is they watched an animated feature.

The morning after the final Montreal performance, I saw the company off at Central Station. The Bolshoi Theatre had booked an entire train to their next destination, Toronto. I waved as they rolled out of the station, and many waved back.

I wasn't surprised to learn a few weeks later that Alexander Godunov defected after a show in New York City. Nor was I surprised that Lyudmila Vlasova opted to stay with the Bolshoi and return to the Soviet Union. She hadn't shared Alexander's interest in the cost of living in North America. To leave your home and family behind is hard. And if that home was the Soviet Union in the 1970s, it was probably much harder, especially for anyone with a high profile.

Alexander Godunov died from alcoholism within fifteen years. As of today, Lyudmila is still going strong.

CHAPTER TWELVE

BROTHERS FROM ANOTHER MOTHER

IN THE EARLY SEVENTIES, DONALD'S car was a purple AMC Javelin that had food-stained, white leatherette upholstery and a reverse gear that didn't work. This flashy "full-speed ahead" car reflected Donald's approach to a lot of things.

His nickname was "The Deke," thanks to business partner Michael Cohl. This was a short form of "DKD", but also referred to a hockey move where a player would fake-out an opponent. However, the name only stuck when Donald was at the beach in a pair of saggy board shorts and a wave knocked him over. He took a tumble and when he stood up, somehow lost his shorts. Inspired by the sight of this large, white, naked man emerging from the water, Michael called out, "Hey look, it's Moby Deke!"

Wherever Donald was at work, the place was usually bustling and noisy. He liked to wheel and deal and "think on his feet." His business partner Terry was the exact opposite.

Terry preferred peace and quiet. He liked to be thoroughly prepared and loved immersing himself in any new contract. He would read the trade magazines from cover to cover. Sass

Jordan's first video had the line in the chorus, "You make me curious, what do you do all day?" Her inspiration was Terry.

And yet these two business partners were perfect for each other. Terry was intensely loyal to Donald, and Donald was especially caring when it came to Terry. Both of them influenced me enormously. No story of my years working at Donald K Donald would be complete without a closer look at Donald and Terry.

ACID-BUDDIES

One day in 1976, Donald and Terry decided, with absolutely no encouragement from me, to experiment with L.S.D.

As a former acid-head, I chose to be a clear-headed companion and keep an eye on the two of them. The last time I ever dropped acid was in 1970. I don't know how many trips I've had; certainly more than 30 and probably less than 50. Most of the time, the tablets or capsules were sold as "mescaline", but I always assumed it was acid mixed with something like Nestle's Quik so it would have an earth-tone vibe. I never had anything close to a "bum trip", although I know a few people who did. I also never had an acid flashback.

In my experience, there are three phases to an acid trip. There is the waiting period. When the first rushes start coming, it's like the cogs are hauling your roller coaster cart up to the highest point on the ride. The fun is in the anticipation. Then there's the free-fall of "peaking." At that point, it's very hard to form a cogent thought, never mind a sentence. If you can direct your mind at all, the one thing to think is "Acid." Whatever else you think is going on, what's really going on is "Acid." Sooner or later, and time is hard to gauge while tripping, the best part of the experience begins. That would be "coming down."

I know this must sound nuts. It's like saying, "I hope I get the flu because I'll feel great once I'm better." But L.S.D. isn't the flu. It's more like your mind falls apart. Then, as it slowly reassembles, you get the sense your entire way of seeing the world is something you control. People even talk about being "re-born." Although I invariably reverted to my old self over the next couple of days, there was this short state of grace when I felt like a new person.

My reason for quitting was simple. It was far too time-consuming. Being stoned for twelve hours is only part of the problem. There are also the next couple of days when it's best if you don't have to make any important decisions. During my college years, I had the luxury of time and Laugh-In was the perfect place to work off an "L.S.D. hang-over." But the next phase of my life required a lot more focus.

On Donald and Terry's first trip I remember a backgammon game in a booth at a bar called Thursday's. Backgammon was a craze at the time and it seemed like everyone was getting into it. But it's not a game where L.S.D. was helpful. You need to roll your dice, remember what you rolled, and then strategically move your discs. When you have trouble even reading the dice, you're off to a shaky start.

A veteran acid tripper might not try anything more challenging than observing the way the pattern in a carpet was moving around. Terry wisely decided to do just that. But Donald was tossing his dice and moving his tiles with gusto. Mind you, he wasn't playing backgammon so much as he was tossing dice and moving the discs, seemingly at random. Before long, Donald was engaged in a loud argument about his ability to count. He would eventually get very good at backgammon, but not on this night.

The second trip saw our intrepid acid buddies at The Moustache. Donald was enjoying the music and pretty lights while Terry decided to chat up a blonde seated at the bar. Clearly, he didn't have his "A-Game" going because the woman took a long draw on her cigarette and blew the smoke in Terry's face.

At that moment, he experienced the kind of transition that might occur in a dream, or an acid trip. Terry was suddenly convinced the building was burning and he had started the fire. Instinct kicked in. He had to save Donald's life. Of course, when Terry suddenly began trying to wrestle Donald out the front door, Donald wrestled back. At that point, the bouncer thought a fight was breaking out but a few of us intervened before anyone got hurt. In the end, Terry succeeded in saving Donald from the great Moustache fire, which never happened. This incident convinced both of them acid was not such a good idea. It also illustrated the dynamic between these two best friends.

LARGER THAN LIFE

Even without mind-altering drugs, Donald was a trip. While Terry would never willingly find himself before a microphone, much less a TV camera, Donald was pretty much the opposite. One time he was presenting Alice Cooper at the arena of the Université de Montreal. That afternoon, a group of about a dozen transvestites in colourful drag turned up and began parading in front of the building. They had placards in English and French bearing the message "Alice Cooper Unfair to Transvestites." It was all just for a laugh.

I thought it was a pretty good joke, and the protesters were certainly having a good time. However, someone in charge of the university's security thought otherwise, took away their placards and dispersed the mock protest just as both the

Channel Twelve Pulse News Cruiser and Donald showed up at the venue.

With no colourful protesters to shoot, the TV news crew had to content themselves with a Donald interview. When asked what happened, his explanation was, "We had these people walking up and down with placards on long poles which could also be used as weapons. To protect the public, the security people moved in and took away their placards. And as we all know, a gay without a pole is easy to take care of." Nobody knew if this was sarcasm or an attempt at a joke. I'm not even sure Donald knew what he meant. But that comment played on both the evening and late-night news.

Another televised event featured Montreal Gazette music reviewer, Juan Rodriguez. Juan wrote a very dismissive review of a Jethro Tull concert. In fact, he conceded that since he'd already seen Jethro Tull a couple of times, he saw no point in suffering through the concert he was supposed to be reviewing. He also suggested the Montreal Forum should be exclusively reserved for hockey games. Donald took strong exception and challenged Juan to a televised debate, again involving Channel Twelve, CFCF-TV.

Surprisingly, Juan accepted the challenge. I say surprisingly because, although Juan Rodriguez possessed an impressive command of written language, he tended to stutter, especially when nervous. Tangling with Donald on live television might not be such a good idea. That night, if the debate was scored by the number of complete words spoken, the final tally might have been Donald: 537 – Juan: 19.

One of Donald's oddest promotions of the seventies was a 3-D television broadcast. Donald made a deal with CFCF-TV where one weekend, they ran a bill of old 3-D horror movies overnight. The station heavily promoted this event and Donald sold the 3-D glasses at Perrette's Milk Stores throughout CFCF's viewing region. These flimsy cardstock frames with one red lens and one blue lens cost a couple of pennies each and sold for a dollar. Even after giving a cut to the convenience stores and splitting the profits with CFCF, Donald earned thousands. Unfortunately, he was only able to run this promotion once because the 3-D effect didn't work. One movie which starred Vincent Price almost seemed three-dimensional at times, but with or without the glasses. The rest of the marathon was a blur and gave people headaches.

Because he always appreciated the importance of money, Donald always provided good value to the sponsors of his shows, especially the ones who paid the most; the breweries. I thought we might have an issue after taking the time to read a Stevie Wonder contract rider. Stevie had very strong views about using his shows to promote alcohol. It was not allowed. When I shared this information with Donald, he smiled and said, "Don't worry. He won't see a thing."

THE END OF AN ERA

I was one of a couple of people who were on the front lines when Donald K Donald developed a ten-province rock concert circuit. But by the end of the decade, the idea of hitting eighty arenas between the Avalon Peninsula and the Alberni Inlet with the same rock group would become a thing of the past.

Part of the reason was, once people saw an international star in a larger market like Moncton, seeing a Canadian band in a smaller market like Newcastle, Amherst or Sussex lost some of its appeal.

A more important reason for the disappearance of the marathon tour (or at least the reason these tours ended so abruptly) was corporate sponsorships. Michael Cohl was always pioneering new ideas for the concert business. In the 1990s he made a deal with the Rolling Stones, utilizing a new model for touring called "The Next Adventure." This marginalized local promoters and eliminated booking agents altogether. It also made a great deal of money for both Michael's company and The Rolling Stones. In the seventies, Michael's best idea might have been selling the commercial sponsorship of concerts. He shared this idea with Donald.

In return for *millions* of dollars each year, Donald committed to insinuating beer and soft drink logos and trademarks wherever possible in connection with his concerts. A typical deal might call for heavy-duty corporate branding involving at least two hundred shows per year. They had to be in larger venues and only nine specified cities mattered. As far as these sponsors were concerned, Canada's most easterly market was now Montreal. In effect, these brewers and soda bottlers suddenly cut Atlantic Canada adrift. Small concert markets all over Canada abruptly ceased to matter in this new age of concert sponsorships.

In the past, one bad show could wipe out the profits from three good ones. A prolonged losing streak could spell real trouble. Under this new plan, Donald could lose ten thousand dollars at every one of the two hundred shows he owed the sponsors, and still clear over a million dollars. Of course, very few of the two hundred shows lost money because, in addition to knowing his business and always doing research, Donald no longer needed to take risks.

The beauty of this plan was apparent to Donald, so he renegotiated the deal he had with his partners and made what seemed like very generous offers to purchase all the shares in "his" company, Donald K Donald Productions. He was about to become rich.

By 1978, I can't say I foresaw the rock concert business was about to go so corporate, or that the tour circuit I had helped to develop was about to vanish. I made my decision to leave touring because I was tired of doing shows.

My imagination had raced ahead of me the first time I headed to a place called "North Battleford." However, the seventh or eighth time you drive into town, you know what the motel room looks, and even smells like. You know by the time the show is over, the only place to eat makes bad pizza and doesn't deliver after eleven. Most of all, you know if you hit the road at nine in the morning, you would still be tidying up fifteen hours later. And this was just an average day.

When I thought of it as fun, it was. But once I thought of it as a job, it was a hard job.

Also, at that point, the Canadian concert industry had consolidated. If you worked for D.K.D., C.P.I. or Perryscope, which effectively were partners, your leverage in negotiating compensation or work assignments was limited. The alternative would be to leave the country or work with a regional promoter which would likely mean working fewer and smaller shows.

I figured a change might be better than a rest, so I asked if I could work in Perryscope's new Vancouver office. But once I learnt that wasn't on the table, I realized what I really wanted was to change my job, not my address.

Donald asked me what I planned on doing. I told him I wanted to work in the record business which would probably mean moving to Toronto. Although I strongly preferred Montreal, I was originally from Southern Ontario and all of my family lived there. I would get used to it pretty quickly.

But before I had time to put together a resume, Terry and Donald approached me with an offer. Aquarius had a new distribution deal with Capitol Records in Toronto. Terry also licensed April Wine to Capitol-EMI for release throughout the rest of the world. He wanted someone to be in charge of marketing and promotion for Aquarius. No one knew the roster better than I did. I'd already been doing the label's radio promotion for years. I was an obvious fit.

Working in the record business opened different channels for advancement. I would get to stay in Montreal. There was a modest salary increase. And Terry and Donald said they wanted me to help look for new talent, which was an important consideration.

But another factor was Donald and Terry had become like family. Our relationship was very friendly but it wasn't founded on friendship. We might find ourselves together socially, but business was usually involved. We didn't share interests or personal friends. And yet we could always rely on each other. Like older brothers who lived their own lives, Donald and Terry only seemed to matter when something actually mattered. At those times they were always there.

EPILOGUE

THE SECOND TIME I SAW the Beatles at Maple Leaf Gardens in 1965, the P.A. consisted of four Traynor columns on each side of the stage. They were likely driven by a 200-watt Bogen amplifier. You could have bought that entire rig, including a couple of Electro-Voice 664 microphones, for under $2000. By the start of the seventies, it was common to count a dozen Altec Lansing Voice of the Theatre cabinets, powered by 1000 watts of amplification, even in a small venue.

Things didn't just get bigger. Before my touring days were over, things had gotten much more technical. For instance, I had to know how much weight the roof beams of the arenas could support and I might have riggers installing winches the night before a show to get all that tonnage aloft. Rock concerts evolved from bands simply playing their music, to becoming spectacles.

But the scale of the production wasn't the only thing that increased. We priced tickets in the early seventies in relation to other music purchases. You could buy a Led Zeppelin album for $4.99 so we priced a ticket to see the band for $6.50. Gradually it dawned on the managers and promoters, since they were selling an experience, it was possible to dramatically increase ticket prices. The term "bucket list" didn't exist in those days. But the industry came to realize, for many people, seeing the Rolling Stones was more like visiting the Grand Canyon than going to a record store; it was something you wanted to do once in your life, and maybe even bring the kids along.

During the first full decade of arena rock, I was in the thick of things. I decided I had enough just as the concert industry was about to get down to serious business. But I don't think I got out too soon. It could be argued the Golden Age of Rock had already happened. The scale of everything seemed to increase, but I'm not sure the quality of the songwriting or the talent improved.

Leaving the concert business didn't mean I was leaving the music business behind. I would spend the next sixteen years at Aquarius Records. Besides seeing the international rise of April Wine (and also how things unraveled), I experienced a wild ride with Corey Hart, and helped develop the recording career of Sass Jordan. Unfortunately, the record business is rarely like a concert where the best is saved for the encore and everyone goes home with a tee-shirt and happy memories.

My years in the record business would have their share of heady victories and bitter setbacks. There would be no shortage of ridiculous situations involving remarkable characters. After the Aquarius years, my career led me to board rooms and back offices. With every passing year, I became more familiar with the artists' contracts and finances, and less involved with artists themselves.

Looking back at that first decade in the concert business, I did exactly what I wanted to do at that time in my life. The sixties was a period when musical eras and influences were colliding. The result was an amazing explosion of creativity. Being a teenager during the sixties was a stroke of good timing I shared with tens of millions of kids my age.

Unlike them, I managed to keep that party going for an additional decade. The music business was good enough to grant me another four decades so I could settle down and devote myself to more normal pursuits like going on a vacation or having a home-life.

I can only think of one lasting after-effect. Many hundreds of times I cued the dimming of house lights, then heard that crowd roar in response. It was often my favourite moment of any given day. I think that's why, for the past forty years, a night seldom goes by when I don't have at least one dream where there's a show about to begin.

ACKNOWLEDGEMENTS

I'M GRATEFUL TO THE MANY people who helped me as I worked on this book. Early encouragement from Oleh Onyfryk, Gary Moffet and Don Breithaupt was very important. I thank Matt Drouin for the freedom to work on the book while also working for a living. Sheila Perkins and Doreen Tang would give me great advice while they also provided their help in the proofing process. The most profound influence on the flow and tone of the book was my editor, Kevin Larken. But I don't think I would have been able to do this without the inspiration and the blessing of Terry and Deke.

CPSIA information can be obtained
at www.ICGtesting.com
Printed in the USA
LVHW080900130920
665255LV00012BA/438/J